Facilitating to Lead!

Ingrid Bens, M.Ed.

Facilitating to Lead!

Leadership Strategies for a Networked World

JOSSEY-BASS
A Wiley Imprint
www.josseybass.com

Published by Jossey-Bass
A Wiley Imprint
989 Market Street, San Francisco, CA 94103-1741   www.josseybass.com

Jossey-Bass books and products are available through most bookstores. To contact Jossey-Bass directly call our Customer Care Department within the U.S. at 800-956-7739, outside the U.S. at 317-572-3986, or fax 317-572-4002.

Jossey-Bass also publishes its books in a variety of electronic formats. Some content that appears in print may not be available in electronic books.

Library of Congress Cataloging-in-Publication Data

Bens, Ingrid.
  Facilitating to lead! : leadership strategies for a networked world / Ingrid Bens.
      p. cm.
  Includes bibliographical references and index.
  ISBN-13: 978-0-7879-7731-3 (pbk.)
  ISBN-10: 0-7879-7731-4 (pbk.)
  1. Teams in the workplace. 2. Group facilitation. 3. Leadership. I. Title.
  HD66.B444 2006
  658.4'092—dc22   2006011518

Printed in the United States of America
FIRST EDITION
PB Printing   10 9 8 7 6 5 4 3 2 1

Contents

Preface

In today's world of back-to-back meetings, there's growing awareness of the vital role that process plays in ensuring effective interaction. The result has been the widespread acceptance of a new and important role in the workplace: that of the meeting facilitator.

Traditionally, leaders have chaired meetings and exerted control over decision making; facilitators stay neutral to ensure that group members take the lead. Until now it has been common practice for the facilitator to be someone other than the group leader and for facilitation to be thought of largely as a meeting tool.

But facilitation has a far greater role to play in today's interactive workplace than simply ensuring the effectiveness of meetings. Given the emerging trends, it's now time for facilitation to emerge from meeting rooms to take its proper place at the center of the leadership function.

A number of factors have converged to create a pressing need for the wholesale adoption of collaborative approaches to leading. The ever expanding deployment of teams, the growing incidence of project-based work, and the rise of the Internet have changed the structure of work. Just as the industrial era ushered in new management forms, the Internet age is now setting the stage for a seismic shift in leader roles.

> The time for facilitative leadership has arrived.

Where factories once needed bosses to oversee orderly production activities, today's networked workplace is in need of ways to stimulate creative thinking, spark innovation, and merge the best ideas. Fortunately the tools that deliver these results have not only been developed, but are accessible to everyone who chooses to learn the facilitator's way.

Before the true value of this tool set can be realized, however, organizations need to shift from thinking about *facilitation* (the noun, which refers to an activity that a designated person performs) to the concept of being *facilitative* (an adjective that describes a new state of being).

When organizations become facilitative, they use the core principles of empowerment and collaboration to shape their corporate culture and their operating principles. They engage key stakeholders in working together to achieve shared goals. They leverage the wisdom and talents of their people to create breakthrough results.

Being facilitative is based on the idea of talking *with* people, not *at* them. It's about creating environments that foster cooperation and link ideas. It's about encouraging creativity so that people can reach higher. It's about moving people to action rather than ordering them to move.

The key step in creating a facilitative workplace is rethinking and reshaping the role of leaders. This begins with realizing that the talents and behaviors that have worked in the past are not likely to be the same ones that will work in the future. The leader who will be most effective in the networked world is the one who can connect with people and spark collective action.

The Purpose and Scope of This Book

This book has been written to support organizations in shifting their mental models of both facilitation and leadership. It aims to help them identify the conditions that need to be in place to support the deployment of facilitative leaders. It also offers leaders practical guidance to aid them during their transformation.

This book is not an overview of core facilitation tools and techniques, which have already been extensively described in dozens of excellent books on the subject. Nor is this book a compilation of the myriad management processes that leaders need to know in order to be effective, since that would be an encyclopedic undertaking.

Instead this book provides a concise outline of the role of the facilitative leader: the core values, the behaviors, the responsibilities, and the main tools. It also discusses the many barriers that can block adoption and suggests strategies that may be helpful in overcoming these. Finally, this book makes the case for the creation of this important new role in the hope of convincing skeptics that the time for this innovation has arrived.

Content Overview

This book is organized into seven chapters with many useful tools and checklists. And there are additional questionnaires in the appendixes.

Chapter One briefly reviews the major forces that have been altering the workplace and the impact of these forces on leadership roles. A definition of facilitative leadership is provided, and that style is compared with other approaches. A checklist of situations where this type of leader is an effective match will help organizations select the right situations for deployment. To make the case for change, both the organizational and personal benefits of facilitative leadership are described.

Chapter Two addresses organizational preparedness for facilitative leadership. Since empowerment is the core issue in the implementation of this style, a four-level model is provided that reframes empowerment from a vague concept to a concrete structuring tool. In an issue related to empowerment, the chapter explores the perceptions of weakness that are often tied to facilitation. The reasons for these perceptions are discussed, as are the generally underestimated powers of the role.

To help organizations prepare for this change, Chapter Two also addresses the main barriers. Buy-in strategies are outlined, as are the key conditions required to support successful deployment. The chapter ends with an organizational readiness assessment, which is supported by an instrument in Appendix A.

Chapter Three focuses on the role of the facilitative leader. It describes the nature of the function in terms of key roles and then compares and contrasts these roles to those played by both traditional leaders and meeting facilitators. The supportive behaviors and the core principles that guide the actions of the facilitative leader are described in this chapter and then translated into an instrument of observable behaviors, which is found in Chapter Five.

To help organizations adjust their hiring criteria, Chapter Three includes a new position description that outlines the core competencies of facilitative leaders. This is followed by a discussion of the core skill of facilitation. The Facilitation Skills Self-Assessment instrument in Appendix B will help leaders assess their level of skill in that area. And to help leaders understand the role more clearly, the chapter features an in-depth exploration of the issues related to assertiveness and authority and specific strategies for negotiating power in a variety of situations.

Chapter Four addresses how any leader can make the transition into the role of facilitative leader. The three ways that organizations can acquire leaders are described and explored in detail to illustrate the many ways these leaders operate. In addition, the chapter outlines the roles and responsibilities of the process specialist as compared to other players in today's networked organization. To clarify questions about the role, there is a section of commonly asked questions. Most of these focus on whether an existing leader can adopt facilitative techniques and play both the process and content expert roles within his or her own team.

Since the success of facilitative leaders depends on the support and cooperation of their teammates, the traditional role of employees is examined and contrasted with the new role that they need to play in support of this transition. The main traits of facilitative partners are described and linked to an instrument of behavioral traits, the Empowered Partner Index, in Chapter Seven.

Chapter Five addresses issues related to the fact that maintaining a collaborative culture requires additional meetings. Since these are meetings that no one has the time to attend, this chapter features strategies to ensure that every meeting is efficient. A dozen unique and highly focused meeting formats are also described, along with tips for improving teleconferences. A section on avoiding meeting problems offers pointers to prevent common meeting pitfalls.

Chapter Six focuses on the distinctive processes that facilitative leaders use to maintain organizational health. The chapter begins by identifying processes that are required at specific stages in the life cycle of a project or team. It then sets out ten essential processes that are hallmark activities for facilitative leaders: new leader integration, visioning, team launch, operational review, survey feedback, after-action debriefing, needs and offers negotiation, peer feedback, mediating interpersonal conflict, and coaching. Each process is described in terms of its purpose, when to use it, main steps, and expected outcomes. Since each of these processes requires additional meetings, suggestions are offered for scheduling these processes to minimize any negative impact.

Chapter Seven provides three performance measurement tools that organizations can use to monitor and evaluate the effectiveness of their facilitative cultures. The first instrument is based on a two-dimensional model that allows facilitative organizations to create a balanced scorecard based on both results and process indicators. The behaviorally based instruments for both the facilitative leader and the empowered partner are in this chapter as well. These tools can be used as the basis of 360-degree feedback activities.

The Epilogue describes life in a facilitative organization that captures the essential impacts of this change.

Facilitative leadership holds out not only the promise of making organizations better, but also offers hope for improving human interactions in a world sorely in need of greater collaboration. These are the types of leaders we both want and need. I hope that this book serves as a valuable resource to those seeking to be part of this important transformation.

June 2006   INGRID BENS
Sarasota, Florida

Acknowledgments

A number of people took precious time from their hectic schedules to add their perspective to this book. I thank Georgie Bishop, performance and learning consultant for the Public Sector Consortium, for adding valuable insight about systems thinking and how much work is being conducted in the white space between organizations; Ellen Gottesdiener, principal consultant of EBG Consulting and author of *Requirements by Collaboration*, for her detailed editing; Bob and Cynthia Vance of Strategics International, for adding several critical components; Richard Nolan, director of education for the VA New England Healthcare System, for his insights about organizational blocks; Mark Vilbert, organization development adviser at Boeing, for helping to ground the book in shop floor realities; Charles K. Bens, author of *Public Sector Performance Measures: Successful Strategies and Tools*, for helping to develop the measurement instruments; James Rollo, organization development consultant with Competitive Advantage Consultants for contributing material about evolving leadership roles; and Michael Goldman, organization development consultant with Facilitation First, for help identifying and describing the essential processes.

I also express special thanks to my first mentor and special friend, Brian Quinn, manager of planning and new programs (retired) at the Human Resources Secretariat for the Ontario Government, Canada, who offered his insights and support not only for this book but for so many of my projects over the past twenty years.

The Author

INGRID BENS is a consultant and trainer whose special areas of expertise are facilitation skills, team building, conflict management, employee participation, and organizational change. She has a master's degree in adult education and more than twenty-five years of experience as a workshop leader and organization development consultant. The workshops she currently conducts address core facilitation skills, advanced facilitation skills, and facilitative leadership strategies. (For information about these workshops, go to www.participative-dynamics.com.)

Bens is the founder of Participative Dynamics, a consulting firm located in Sarasota, Florida, and a founding partner in Facilitation First located in Toronto, Canada. Bens is also the author of *Facilitating with Ease!* (2nd ed., Jossey-Bass, 2005) and *Advanced Facilitation Strategies* (Jossey-Bass, 2005).

1

THE LEADERSHIP CONTEXT

Leaders who operate in today's networked world of projects and teams find themselves in a dynamic environment that didn't exist just a few decades ago. Where managers once oversaw functions they had previously performed themselves, today's leaders often head up diverse groups of specialists whose areas of expertise are not familiar to them. Where supervisors traditionally worked in close proximity to their staff, today's employees may be located hundreds or even thousands of miles away. Where bosses once wielded absolute authority over compliant workers, today's leaders often work with independent colleagues over whom they have little or no authority.

Although many organizations continue to operate in the traditional mode, the incidence of geographically dispersed workers and lateral structures is on the rise. Today even the most conservative, hierarchical organizations are permeated with technology implementation teams, process improvement projects, new product partnerships, and interorganizational networks. The people who head up these groups find themselves facing unique challenges. These leaders quickly discover that being effective on a succession of complex projects requires a new set of skills and techniques.

When asked to describe what a leader is, most people will say something like: "someone who's in charge," "the person who's accountable," or "the one who has the final say." This command-and-control notion of leadership has been with us for centuries and is pervasive. But in the world of projects and teams, this conventional approach to leading is no longer effective.

People who head up projects staffed with knowledge workers know this. Team leaders know it as well, as do managers whose boomer-age workforce is being replaced by younger workers with different expectations. In every sector of the economy, changing organizational patterns combined with shifts in worker attitudes are ushering in a dynamic new style.

The Transforming Workplace

Over the past several decades, a number of major forces have been altering the workplace. The globalization of markets, the large-scale application of technology, the drive for total quality, the need for superior customer service, and the demand for innovation have all been exerting enormous adaptive pressures.

In response to these trends, organizations of all sizes have been adjusting their structures. Instead of being organized purely by specialty departments such as quality control, human resources, and marketing, many organizations have integrated these functions into networks that are focused on specific customers, products, or market segments.

Where work was once conducted largely within departments, more and more innovative and important work is now being conducted in the matrix, or space between departments and organizations. This change has many positive features: the work is often more challenging and dynamic, people are afforded the opportunity of working with colleagues from diverse backgrounds, and ideas are shared across traditional boundaries.

> *Matrix:* the substance in which elements are embedded; a network of interconnected elements; the space between elements; a network of partners.

Matrix Work Is Different

While work within organizational boundaries tends to be ongoing, matrix work is typically carried out as time-limited projects. While staff inside departments are more likely to be long term, project team workers know that their assignments are temporary. Rather than report to a single supervisor or manager, matrix workers often report to more than one management authority.

One of the main reasons organizations deploy matrix teams is to create a blend of talents capable of breakthrough thinking. When matrix networks are made up of the right knowledge workers, they allow organizations to forge synergistic partnerships and create innovative products.

There are other advantages as well. Rather than being task driven, matrix teams are more likely to be goal driven. They are also more likely to be composed of knowledge workers who have been selected for their specialized expertise and capacity to contribute to the achievement of a specific goal.

On the most elementary level, a knowledge worker is someone who possesses advanced knowledge and is hired to apply that expertise. Some knowledge workers are easy to spot. These are the people with advanced degrees in specialty areas, like scientists, engineers, medical researchers, and software designers.

But there are lots of other knowledge workers who are harder to spot. If we broaden the definition to include those who need to be skillful and use their deductive abilities on the job, then the number of workers who fit into this category expands exponentially. In this context, every salesperson, every customer service representative, and every shop floor worker has knowledge that's important to the success of their respective organizations.

Considering the rate at which unskilled jobs either disappear or continue to migrate offshore, it may not be an overstatement to say that a growing proportion of the employment remaining in developed nations is knowledge work.

Examples of Matrix Networks

Many knowledge workers continue to operate within traditional departments, but a growing number work in groups located in the space between departments. There are countless examples of these matrix structures in every industry and within every sector:

- Teams of managers and external consultants navigating a complex merger or acquisition
- Technology implementation committees composed of technology experts and end users
- Process improvement initiatives made up of engineers, managers, and manufacturing staff
- Coordinating committees made up of managers and specialists from a variety of departments or agencies working together to implement a new policy or program
- Most schools where principals coordinate the efforts of teams of teachers who autonomously manage their classrooms
- Cooperative teams established by former competitors to win and then manage large contracts that are too complex for any one of them to manage on their own
- New business start-up projects composed of specialists drawn from a variety of schools, government agencies, and private firms

> More and more work is being conducted in the space between organizations.

This way of organizing work has become particularly widespread in scientific, engineering, and technology firms where it's now common for staff to spend more time working on a succession of projects than working within any particular department.

Changing Workforce Expectations

At the same time that organizations have been transforming, employees have been changing. Decades of higher education and personal autonomy have altered worker outlooks and expectations.

In the 1950s workers were looking for steady employment, a fair salary, and opportunities for advancement. This was the nine-to-five world of clear job descriptions and stable work assignments. Workers could expect to put in their hours and go home to focus on their family and other interests. The worker of the 1950s was accustomed to the hierarchical nature of the workplace and expected leaders to be directive and authoritative.

Members of Generation X and younger have grown up in a radically different culture than even the baby boomers, who currently dominate the workplace. These younger workers have known constant change and are accustomed to working in teams. Unlike their parents, they don't expect lifelong employment.

> Today's workers are accustomed to greater personal autonomy than previous generations.

Instead of permanence, they're more interested in finding meaningful work that features opportunities to learn and grow. They also expect to be personally engaged at work; they want to control their workday and have a voice in important decisions that affect them.

Technology Matters

Surely the most significant change of the past few decades has been the impact of technology, which has radically altered every aspect of how people do their work. The arrival of the personal computer made it possible for employees to access a world of information, create complex personal networks, and conduct work across distances.

In contrast to employees of the 1950s, who were dependent on their manager for corporate information, today's wired employees can access business data and read the latest news on the company intranet. Where employees once had to gain approval to communicate with colleagues outside their department, information now whizzes back and forth across organizational boundaries.

Technology has also changed the structure of work. Today's knowledge workers can operate from anywhere and at any hour using their laptops and cell phones. Teleconferences have replaced many meetings, a trend that's going to grow as videoconferencing technology becomes more widespread. It is no longer unheard of for team members to work on a project for months without ever having a face-to-face meeting.

The Transforming Workplace	
From	*To*
Stable departments	Shifting networks of teams
Vertical hierarchies	Lateral matrices
Task orientation	Goal orientation
Homogeneous staff groupings	Diverse skill sets
Geographically close	Geographically scattered
Communications dependent	Personally networked
Leaders know the work	Leaders may not know the work
9 to 5	24/7
Information dependent	Widely networked
Operating without technology	Totally wired
Expectations of lifelong	Expectations of autonomy employment and personal growth

Implications for Leaders

The combined effect of these trends is changing what it means to be a leader in today's world of work:

• When employees don't know as much about the content of their work as their supervisors and managers, it's appropriate and effective for these leaders to direct the details of staff efforts. But when team members are experts in specialty areas that are unknown to the leader, it is impossible for the leader to direct staff efforts.

• When employees work in centralized locations, the leader can monitor employee efforts during preset hours of operation. But when team members work in remote locations and set their own timetable for achieving personal deadlines, the leader is in no position to judge staff effectiveness through direct observation.

• When the leader has direct control over the budget and the hiring and firing of staff, he or she has the authority to control workload assignments and discipline staff. But when team members are assigned to a team or committee in which both staffing and budgets are controlled elsewhere, the leader has few levers to control member actions.

• When staff roles are narrowly defined and feature repetitious tasks, it's often appropriate for the leader to provide oversight to ensure that work gets done. But when the work demands creativity and innovation and results depend on people taking initiative, close oversight is futile and serves only to undermine individual initiative.

Just as the advent of the industrial age created the need for new approaches to managing work, the proliferation of matrix structures is creating the need for a transformation in the role of the leader. This change also represents an opportunity for leadership thinking to make a quantum leap forward by taking on the form that reflects the dimensions of the Internet age.

Leaders in Matrix Networks

- Instead of dealing largely with individuals, they work with people in groups.
- Instead of supervising hours of operation and measuring workload, they help staff identify parameters within which they can become self-managing.
- Instead of directing tasks, they motivate people to achieve superior results.
- Instead of directing the mission, they align team efforts with organizational goals.

The Overlooked Tool Set

For leaders searching for strategies to manage these new realities, there's good news. The leadership style that's most effective in this setting has already been developed and refined. It is known as facilitative leadership.

Facilitation is a process through which a person helps others work effectively. It draws out the knowledge of group members in order to achieve superior results. It values everyone's contribution, shares power, and instills ownership. Facilitators help groups improve the quality and quantity of their work by getting members to work together more effectively.

The facilitator is one of the most important roles to emerge in the modern workplace. It was developed in the middle of the twentieth century as a blend of management theory and applied behavioral science. It was created in order to engage and empower followers so that their expertise and knowledge would be fully used.

> The tools and techniques that matrix leaders need can be found in facilitation.

Of all the skill sets that support the shift from the traditional, directive mode to the style most needed by matrix leaders, none is more relevant than the role of facilitator.

What Is Facilitative Leadership?

Facilitative leadership is a skilled approach to leading that's based on the core beliefs and practices of group facilitation. It makes extensive use of process tools in order to provide structure and casts the leader in the role of helper and enabler.

Facilitative leaders share the core beliefs of facilitation:

- People are intelligent and capable, and they want to do the right thing.
- Everyone's opinion has value, regardless of an individual's rank or position.
- Groups can make better decisions than individuals acting alone.
- People are more committed to the ideas and plans that they create.
- People will take responsibility and assume accountability for their actions and can become partners in the enterprise.

- The role of the leader is to evoke the best possible performance from each member of their team.

The ultimate goal of the facilitative leader is to develop the leadership talents of others by instilling confidence, authority, and responsibility in each person. They aim to create organizations that are participative, responsive, and essentially self-managing, exactly the kind of workplace in which knowledge workers thrive.

To place facilitative leadership in context, it may be helpful to compare it to the leadership styles of traditional directive leaders.

Traditional Directive Leaders

This is the traditional command-and-control style that was created for a bygone era when a great deal of work was deliberately reduced to its simplest components and mechanized. This leader sets the direction, has the final word, and is personally held accountable. The style is based on the assumption that the leader is the most knowledgeable and experienced person in the group and should therefore exert control over the important aspects of the operation. In this mode, followers are viewed as less capable than the leader and in need of both direction and control.

Directive leaders have a high involvement with the content of the work being performed but have a relatively low involvement in the relationship elements. In other words, they spend most of their time ensuring that their people know what to do, place less emphasis on developing staff relationships or personal capabilities, and typically have the power to hire, fire, or redeploy their people and have the final word in major decisions.

Traditional directive leaders:

- Are task focused
- Set direction and make strategic decisions
- Control work assignments
- Work with people individually

- Control information
- Retain the right to make decisions
- Place a minor emphasis on people skills
- Have rank and privileges
- Relate in a distant and formal style
- Communicate down
- Hold few meetings
- Rarely give or receive feedback
- Feel that staff work for them
- Retain accountability for outcomes
- Work to meet the expectations of their managers

The directive mode is effective where the leader possesses expertise that is essential to the operation and when staff members need both direction and oversight in order to do their jobs.

Today's More Engaging Leaders

Over the past few decades, most workplaces have become more informal. In addition, managers and supervisors have been sensitized to age group, gender, and diversity issues. Many have worked on teams and have developed their meeting and group membership skills. These leaders are communicative and people savvy. They're more relaxed in their approach and tend to be more willing to engage than the classic command-and-control boss is. They're good listeners and know how to ask probing questions. They're participative and support the value of teamwork.

Today's more engaging leaders are still highly involved with directing tasks, but they combine this with an increased focus on both improving how work gets done and enhancing interpersonal relations. Although they're more process focused, these leaders continue to be primarily accountable for the results that their people achieve.

This approach to leading is very effective when leaders have sufficient expertise to be in a position to evaluate and direct the work of their staff. It is also the desired approach to take when staff members lack total proficiency and need development. Many of today's leaders are very effective operating in this high involvement style.

Thus, in contrast to traditional directive leaders, today's more engaging leaders:

- Are open, informal, and friendly
- Possess interpersonal skills
- Value teamwork and collaboration
- Are customer focused and quality conscious
- Are interested in continuous learning
- Are willing to engage and empower their people
- Have meeting management skills
- Are receptive to change
- Are communicative and open to feedback
- Are highly involved in improving both work processes and staff capabilities
- Are still involved in directing tasks
- Remain accountable for results
- Still feel that staff work for them
- Still work to meet the expectations of their managers

Supervisors and managers who exhibit these traits are well on their way to being facilitative leaders and often think that they're already there. But true facilitative leadership requires a further shift.

The Traits of Facilitative Leaders

True facilitative leaders are more than just people savvy; they're group process focused. They not only hold meetings to gain staff input, they know how to structure every type of conversation to ensure effective collaboration. They do more than delegate; they systematically empower. They are not only open to employee input; they deliberately structure activities to ensure that staff evaluate them and each other on a regular basis.

Leaders who operate in this mode deliberately leave content matters to group members while they focus their energy on building effective partnerships and networks. They also focus on providing the enabling structures that support superior performance. Rather than coming to meetings to make decisions, these leaders provide decision-making structures. Rather than deciding strategy, identifying priorities, and assigning responsibilities, they provide the right structuring tools so that members can create those plans for themselves. Rather than make things happen, they enable others to get things done. They are helpers and enablers.

Although this style is not applicable to all situations, it is the right approach for groups whose members are capable of both making effective decisions and working independently. It's ideally suited for projects and teams where the leader is coordinating the efforts of competent specialists whose work he or she isn't in a position to understand. This style is also relevant for any work group where members are highly skilled and accountable for outcomes. Any leader can shift to the facilitative mode once his or her staff possess the capacity to work independently and assume responsibility for outcomes.

Facilitative leaders:

- Firmly believe in the principles of collaboration and participation
- Are master facilitators who are familiar with an extensive set of organizing tools
- Systematically empower in order to transfer content control to their staff
- Strive to build collaborative decisions based on staff input
- Possess and use high-level interpersonal skills like active lis-

tening, questioning, and paraphrasing when interacting with others

- Understand how to build and maintain high-performance teams
- Are excellent communicators who freely share information
- Operate without status or rank consciousness
- Focus on continuous improvement of both the work and the operation
- Actively engage in giving and receiving feedback
- Train and coach their people
- Manage conflict and mediate disputes skillfully
- Share accountability for outcomes with team members
- Work to meet the expectations of stakeholders, including their staff

The Need for Versatility

While each approach to leading has its place, it's critically important that every leader be capable of variable styles. Leaders who acquire facilitative skills will gain the versatility of being able to operate in a process-oriented mode in some settings while retaining a task-oriented approach in other situations.

> All leaders need to be capable of operating in both modes: the task-focused directive mode for situations where close oversight of tasks is needed and is workable and the process-focused mode to provide structure when leading teams of experts.

Without the ability to shift to the process mode, leaders will be compelled to use a directive approach even in situations where it doesn't work. This is now happening in many organizations where projects are being managed by controlling leaders who end up micromanaging their highly skilled colleagues when what is really needed is process support.

Organizational Benefits of Deploying Facilitative Leaders

Facilitative leadership holds the promise of being the foremost leadership strategy for the networked world. When organizations deploy skilled process specialists to lead their projects and teams, they reap a number of significant benefits:

- When operational elements are continuously reviewed and improved, the overall effectiveness of the operation increases.
- When meetings are highly structured and assertively facilitated, dialogue becomes important and valuable.
- When employee ideas and active involvement are sought, there's more collaboration and innovation.
- When staff members are empowered and supported, creativity and innovation increase.
- When staff are treated as valued colleagues, commitment and motivation increase.
- When teams are carefully managed through their development stages, more teams attain the high-performance state.

Personal Benefits of Shifting Styles for Leaders

Supervisors and managers who feel that they're operating effectively when they control tasks and are the main decision makers will naturally wonder why they should bother changing. Here are some of the benefits related to adopting a facilitative approach:

- The increased ability to help others make complex collaborative decisions
- Enhanced capacity to build and maintain healthy teams
- Greater use of staff resources
- Staff who are more engaged and more responsible for their actions and for finding and solving problems

- Shared accountability for results
- Greater commitment and buy-in through input and involvement
- Team members who are more self-managing
- A more collegial and participative culture
- An expanded tool kit for managing group dynamics and leveraging staff resources

Perhaps the greatest gain is that staff in a participative environment act more like leaders themselves. Not only does this approach share the burden of responsibility, but it also creates a rich source of leaders for the entire organization.

> One definition of a leader: someone who creates leaders.

Making the Match

Facilitative leadership is not the right approach for every situation, but it is right for situations that feature most of the traits in the following checklist. Use this checklist to determine if your project or team is in need of this type of leader:

- ❑ The group consists of strong subject matter experts who need to align around new organizational goals and outcomes.
- ❑ Individuals with different performance measurement systems need to work together to produce a collective outcome.
- ❑ The group has been charged with the responsibility of achieving specific results that require initiative, innovation, and creativity.
- ❑ The group needs to become a cohesive team and periodically meet to maintain and improve team effectiveness.
- ❑ Group members will be held personally accountable for the extent to which they contribute to the achievement of specified results.

❑ Individual members are required to be self-motivated and self-managing because they work independently.

❑ The members have access to technology and can communicate freely across organizational boundaries.

❑ The group is dealing with challenges such as collaborating between historically hostile parties or dealing with complex bureaucracies.

❑ The decisions being made by group members require broad support and commitment from key stakeholders.

❑ Some of the decisions that the team will need to make are extremely complex and sensitive.

❑ High levels of collaboration will be needed to arrive at solutions that have the commitment of a diverse set of stakeholders.

❑ The leadership position has been designed without traditional levers of power and control, or the leader is operating without direct authority over some or all of the members.

❑ The complexity of the situation or past history calls for the presence of a leader who is seen to be neutral by all parties.

❑ The situation periodically requires that the leader manage conflicts or negotiate between parties who are at odds.

2

PREPARING THE WORKPLACE FOR FACILITATIVE LEADERSHIP

Once the need for facilitative leaders has been determined, it is vitally important that the right conditions be put into place to support this new role. First and foremost, organizations must ensure that both facilitative leaders and their teams are properly empowered to be able to function effectively.

When empowerment first came to notice in the 1980s, it captured a lot of attention and quickly became a major buzzword. Sadly, it fell out of style as quickly as it had come into vogue. This happened when people became disillusioned by the gap between the rhetoric about empowerment and the reality of how decisions were actually being made.

The cause of this early disillusionment often stemmed from the lack of structure used to clearly define power relationships. Instead of identifying what empowerment meant in different situations, people got caught up in the *idea* of empowerment. Not only that, but when the gurus talked about empowerment, different groups heard different things.

When upper managers heard the word, they thought it meant that employees were going to take on more work and accept greater responsibility for results. When employees heard about empowerment, they tended to think that it meant they were going to be given free rein to make important decisions and implement actions. This gap in interpretation often made employees feel that management was not walking the talk about teams.

> The term *empowerment* has developed a negative image.

17

The fact that *empowerment* has become a word with negative connotations is most unfortunate, since empowerment is the centerpiece of the facilitative approach to leading. To the facilitative leader, empowerment is not a vague, philosophical concept but a structured tool that ensures that the talents of all stakeholders are fully used.

If there is one major difference between traditional and facilitative leadership styles, it revolves around how each style manages empowerment. Directive leaders maintain control over content and reserve the right to make decisions. They feel accountable for results and operate with low levels of empowerment. In contrast, facilitative leaders intentionally operate at high empowerment levels to ensure that accountability is shared and that decisions are made by the individuals most capable of making them.

To create an atmosphere in which top-down control doesn't stifle innovation or stall progress, organizations need to centralize and standardize only what needs to be managed that way and then empower their people to decide all the rest. Organizations that don't accept increased employee participation won't be able to get the best ideas out of their people, hang on to their talent, or become leaders in their field.

> Empowerment stops being a vague concept when it's properly structured.

One way to reduce both the risks and the fears that empowerment will lead to a loss of control is to take a structured approach. Since the concept of empowerment is so prone to misunderstanding, it's important to use a clear empowerment model to bring structure and clarity to the concept.

The Four-Level Empowerment Model

There are four levels to decision making. The key to understanding this model is to recognize that each of the four levels has its place depending on the capabilities of the group and the nature of the decision.

The Four-Level Empowerment Grid summarizes the levels and their empowerment. The box at the top of the grid represents all of the power in any given situation. The diagonal line indicates how power is divided between management and staff.

Four-Level Empowerment Grid

			Staff Role
Management Role			
Level I: Directive Style	Level II: Consultative Style	Level III: Participative Style	Level IV: Delegative Style
Management decides and then informs staff	Management decides after consulting staff	Staff recommend and act after receiving approval	Staff decide and act (preapproval)
Appropriate situations			
Information is sensitive, staff lack skills or experience, or accountability can't be shared	Accountability can't be shared but management wishes input from staff	Staff ideas and active participation are desired, but risk is high or members lack experience to go it alone	Staff have the needed skills and can assume full accountability for outcomes
Effect			
Management control and accountability; staff are dependent	Management benefits from staff ideas; staff are more involved than at level I	Staff take initiative and implement outcomes; management and staff are interdependent	Staff take responsibility and are independent

Level I: Directive Style

This level is used in to situations in which management will make a decision without consulting with staff. Management then informs the affected parties, who are expected to comply with the decision. This is a directive decision and is appropriate in these situations:

- Both knowledge and accountability reside solely with management.
- There are legal or other nonnegotiable elements.
- The matter has confidential aspects, accountability can't be shared, or severe time limits make collaboration impossible.

At this level, staff are not involved in the decision but are expected to comply with it. This is the least complex way to make a decision, but lacks both input and buy-in, and encourages a workforce that waits to be told what to do.

Level II: Consultative Style

Level II empowerment refers to situations when management reserves the right to make a decision but wishes to gain staff input first. Employees are asked for their ideas but are made aware that the decision will be made by management, who will then inform them of the decision, with which they're expected to comply.

This is therefore a consultative approach. A consultative approach is effective when employees have information that will improve outcomes. Consulting staff is relatively easy and increases buy-in.

Level III: Participative Style

Level III empowerment refers to situations in which staff are asked to recommend a course of action, but management approval is required before taking action.

This is a participative approach and is most appropriate when staff have knowledge about the situation and their active involvement is needed for implementation. It engages staff and makes use of their ideas. Although management retains final authority to make decisions, staff involvement and buy-in levels are high.

Level IV: Delegative Style

Level IV empowerment refers to situations where staff are given full authority to make a specific decision, create action steps, and implement those plans without further approvals from the management.

This is a delegated decision. The approach is most effective when employees have demonstrated their capacity and willingness to assume full responsibility for a specific matter. This approach leverages group resources and assigns accountability to group members. Level IV empowerment encourages a workforce to be responsible and self-managing.

Using the Model

Facilitative leaders analyze each task or decision in terms of its difficulty, inherent risks, and the capability of group members to make an effective decision. They then choose the most appropriate empowerment level based on this assessment.

If decision-making responsibility can't be shared or if group members lack the ability to make a particular decision, then the empowerment level for that decision will remain at level I or II. If decision-making responsibility can be shared and group members are capable, the decision can be moved to level III or IV.

Once this model is shared throughout an organization, it's possible for everyone to have clear and responsible conversations about empowerment. Upper management can set and then adjust empowerment levels, decision by decision, based on the strengths of various teams. Teams can periodically make their case for increases or decreases in empowerment concerning specific items.

With this model, empowerment goes from being a vague and even unsettling idea to an important structuring tool for managing and adjusting the culture of any organization. Leaders who operate in the directive mode rely heavily on levels I and II in order to maintain control over content. In contrast, facilitative leaders strive to shift decision making to levels III and IV in order to tap into the expertise of group members.

Facilitative leaders use the empowerment model as a platform to construct a detailed log that lists all of the decisions affecting their team—for example, setting budgets, assigning roles, hiring teammates, purchasing equipment, and organizing the work space. The team then uses their log to identify individual items where they feel they need to negotiate increases or decreases in decision-making authority (see the Sample Empowerment Planning Chart). The facilitative leader is continuously clarifying and helping the members adjust empowerment levels, which are then published so that those outside the team understand their authority.

How Much Empowerment Is Enough?

When an organization wants to increase employee accountability, it is essential to raise decision-making empowerment to the highest level possible. Most level I decisions can be elevated to at least level II, since consultations are relatively simple to conduct through focus groups, online questionnaires, and surveys.

In many situations, level III empowerment is a wise choice since staff ideas are taken into account and they take the lead in implementation. This empowerment level will be especially appealing to organizations with issues about sharing control. Shifting to level III represents a positive step toward creating a shared accountability culture. Nevertheless, there are two major problems with overusing level III. The first is a matter of efficiency. Imagine a multinational organization with hundreds of projects and teams, each of which has had its empowerment topped out at level III. Pic-

Sample Empowerment Planning Chart

	Level I	Level II	Level III	Level IV
Budget allocation	X			
Budget management			X	
Establishing parameters		X		
Setting objectives			X	
Setting time lines	X			
Creating milestones			X	
Identifying responsibilities				X
Work planning				X
Product changes			X	
Meeting management				X
Hiring colleagues				X
Performance appraisals				X

ture activity on each of these teams grinding to a halt while piles of recommendations sit in a bottleneck waiting for management approval. The second problem with an overuse of level III empowerment is that it discourages groups from becoming more capable and accountable. Any organization that deploys teams in order to seek efficiency and innovation needs to be sensitive to the fact that those teams invariably need to be granted greater freedom to be creative and act autonomously.

> Matrix networks must operate at higher empowerment levels in order to be effective.

Correcting Perceptions of Weakness

One of the unintended consequences of increasing empowerment levels is that it creates the illusion that facilitative leaders are largely powerless. What many observers miss is that these leaders increase their control over work management processes to such an extent that they become very influential. The problem is that old paradigm definitions are being used to define what power means.

This perception of weakness also stems largely from the fact that few people have seen a truly accomplished process specialist in a leadership position. Those who have know that process leaders are assertive and possess an abundance of power, but this power is located in other areas.

Instead of controlling what happens, facilitative leaders are in command of how things get done. They provide so much structure and are so assertive at managing the relationship elements of their teams and their initiatives that their colleagues inevitably view them as anything but weak. Chapter Three contains examples of how these leaders use process control, as well as strategies for gaining leverage, to greatly strengthen the power of this role.

> Erroneous perceptions of facilitation are blocking its widespread adoption.

Perhaps the biggest perceptual barrier to facilitative leadership is the old notion that anything to do with teams and facilitation is that "touchy-feely stuff" that's aimed at creating a "warm and fuzzy" workplace. This view arose in the early days of teams and still lingers in the minds of many. It is a view that will be fully and finally erased only when organizations grasp how critically important high-level process skills are to the overall success of their most important initiatives.

The Durability of the Directive Mode

Despite the fact that the structure of work has been transformed and employee attitudes have shifted, leadership styles in most organizations have barely budged out of the directive mode. Certainly there are more teams, and today's employees participate more in decision making than ever before, but anyone who works in a large organization, even ones that have lots of teams, know that top-down, directive leadership styles are alive and well at every level.

The hardiness of the command-and-control approach should come as no real surprise, since it's been dominant for tens of thousands of years. There are complex reasons that this approach is still widespread, even in situations where it's no longer a good fit. Rising pressure to perform faster than the competition, for example, creates an atmosphere in which a "tell them what to do so we can just get it done" approach seems most practical. In this environment, quick fixes are justified, often without regard for long-term implications.

To most people, the concept of a leader who's not making content decisions fails to conform to the accepted model of the leader who is in control and always makes the decisions. The image of a supervisor or manager who deliberately engages his or her people in decision making represents a major paradigm shift.

In addition, there are challenges related to how facilitation is perceived. Since most facilitation takes place in meetings, it's commonly viewed as a meeting tool. As a result, most managers have seen it operating only in that context and have no frame of reference about how it could serve them if they used it to underpin their daily operating style.

Since facilitators are usually neutral outsiders, it's easy to see why leaders view the role as being more appropriate for external consultants and human resource specialists. As a result, when most managers hear the term *facilitator*, they don't think it applies to them.

> Viewing facilitation as being only about better meetings misses its real potential as a powerful management tool.

Since the deployment of facilitative leaders is a major cultural shift, it's important to identify and address the many impediments to its wholesale adoption:

- When decision-making power is shared, the leader relinquishes control over outcomes.

- Participative decision making is far more complex and time-consuming than solo decision making.

- Teams are relationship intense and prone to periodic episodes of storming that calls for careful management.

- Some individuals are not psychologically or emotionally well suited to managing in a relationship-intense manner.

- Two-way communication requires willingness not only to listen but also to act on the information that's received.

- Coaching individuals and mediating conflicts are stressful and time-consuming activities.

- Feedback activities require openly admitting flaws, then taking the time to implement improvement suggestions.

- Most supervisors and managers lack the group process skills that are the cornerstone of this approach, since these competencies have not previously been considered essential core practices for leaders.

Overcoming Barriers to Process

All facilitative leaders need to be sensitive to the fact that most organization are already awash in such an abundance of process that the idea of yet more process is sure to be resisted. This means that facilitative leaders need to carefully explain the need for the processes they will be adding and explicitly negotiate agreement from team members to take part in the conversations that are central to this approach to leading. It is vitally important to gain explicit agreement to conduct these additional process activities at the start of the relationship to avoid resistance and push-back at a later date.

Facilitative leadership is a major departure from past practices.

Although process management activities have been around for decades, they have not been widely adopted by traditional hierar-

Comparing Cultures	
Most Traditional Cultures Already:	*Most Traditional Cultures Still Don't:*
Establish outcome measures	Engage staff in strategic goal setting
Hold team-building sessions	Engage staff in creating cultural norms
Measure performance outputs	Monitor and manage team effectiveness
Conduct after-action debriefings	Regularly conduct operational reviews
Conduct performance appraisals	Negotiate shifts in empowerment
Conduct climate surveys	Hold regular survey feedback sessions
Coach and mentor staff	Ask staff to appraise their leaders
	Routinely tune up their teams
	Use peer feedback and peer counseling

chical organizations. Even organizations that deploy hundreds of teams don't use many of them. Facilitative leaders need to be aware of the three main reasons that these processes are resisted:

- *Time pressure.* Process discussions are unproductive in the sense that they use up precious time that would otherwise be spent working on the task. This is time no one can afford to give up. Key players at each level need to be convinced that time spent on process-related activities will in fact improve productivity.
- *Fear.* Conversations in which people give and receive feedback or critique the work of others are threatening and

unsettling. People worry that their comments will have reper-
cussions. Relationships can be made worse. Facilitators always
need to realistically assess the risk level of conversations and
ensure that the appropriate rules, called *safety norms*, are in
place before launching into feedback discussions in order to
keep everyone safe.

- *Perception*. Process conversations that focus on relationship
  elements are often seen as that "soft, touchy-feely stuff" that's
  nice to do but not essential. Facilitators need to address those
  perceptions by identifying the upside of managing relationships and regularly reporting on the benefits.

Buy-In Strategies

One way to overcome these barriers is to engage both upper managers and team members in a conversation about benefits and consequences. This is done by holding a discussion based on two
related questions:

> "What are the benefits of operational reviews, meeting effec-
> tiveness surveys, peer reviews, team effectiveness surveys,
> conflict mediations, and after-action debriefings?"

> "What are the consequences of *not* taking time to monitor
> and continuously improve these processes?"

The ensuing discussion will help generate buy-in to this major cultural change.

Once key players have granted their approval for these activities, facilitators must take care to avoid losing that agreement. They
can do this by periodically surveying members about the effectiveness of the time they have spent tending to process and track their
responses for later reporting. (See the Sample Effectiveness Survey.)

Facilitative leaders can demonstrate their sensitivity to these
barriers by designing all processes to be as time effective and safe as
possible. Of course, it's of paramount importance that the time they

SAMPLE EFFECTIVENESS SURVEY

1. To what extent do you feel that the discussions about team effectiveness, relationships, and how we operate were worthwhile?

1	2	3	4	5
No value	A little value	Not sure	Very valuable	Essential

2. To what extent do you feel that time spent discussing operational effectiveness saved time in the long run?

1	2	3	4	5
A lot of time was wasted	A little time was wasted	It's a draw	A bit of time was saved	A lot of time was saved

3. To what extent did process conversations affect the outcomes achieved by our team?

1	2	3	4	5
Adversely affected outcomes	Some affected effects	Not sure	Some positive effects	Positively affected outcomes

spend on facilitative process discussions never exceeds the time they spend facilitating task-related activities.

A note of caution: facilitative leaders should never let themselves be pressured into abandoning important process discussions. Attempting to operate without the ability to conduct the activities that monitor and correct the operation will reduce the facilitative leader to running work planning and regular staff meetings, powerless to correct whatever goes wrong with the team.

The Importance of Organizational Support

Once organizations fully recognize the critical importance of process specialists to the success of their enterprise, they will be compelled to find ways to overcome various obstacles.

A good starting point is for upper managers to sensitize themselves to the dimensions of the facilitative leadership role so that they can identify the specific projects and teams in need of this form of leadership. They also need to examine the organization's culture and recognize that adjustments will be required. If strategic decisions are currently made without staff input, if the organization operates with low empowerment levels, or if leaders have never experienced upward feedback, these practices will need to be adjusted.

Most organizations will need to add job descriptions that reflect the traits of the process specialist role. The generic list of key competencies that is provided in the next chapter may be helpful in creating new position parameters.

Once these kinds of leaders are in place, the criteria by which they're personally evaluated, compensated, and promoted also need to be amended to ensure that these leaders aren't judged by traditional standards and graded unfairly. An index of observable traits helpful in forming the basis of an upward feedback mechanism is also provided in the next chapter.

> Upper managers need to become more facilitative to model the way.

Finally, these types of leaders need upper managers who are ready to adjust their own leadership style to one that's more collaborative and inclusive. Top-level leaders who continue to operate in the "do as I say" mode will find that their behaviors undermine the cultural message that facilitative leaders send their staff.

Implementation Strategies

Even when the need for facilitative leadership has been recognized, it's often a difficult change to put in place. One strategy is to create an implementation plan that phases in deployment over a number of years.

A key part of a gradual strategy in many large organizations is the creation of an internal cadre of facilitators. In most cases, participation in these cadres is open to anyone interested in gaining facilitation skills. There are organizations where candidates for promotion to leadership roles are required to serve a term on the facilitator cadre.

Once cadre members have received facilitation training, they are made available to assist any group in the organization that requests their services. These internal facilitators typically conduct from ten to twenty facilitations a year and serve an average of two years. During that time, the effectiveness of internal facilitators is monitored to allow the organization to identify individuals who have the potential to become facilitative leaders.

Gradually phasing facilitators into an organization allows time for both skill building and adjustment. Each stage can take months or even years to complete. Here is an example of a graduated implementation plan that features the deployment of an internal cadre:

Stage 1

- Sensitization to the nature of the role
- Creation of facilitation skills workshops
- Skill building for existing leaders
- Encouraging leaders to facilitate their staff meeting

Stage 2

- Creation of a cadre of internal facilitators
- Offering facilitation assistance to groups by request
- Development of facilitative leader position description

Stage 3

- Identification of situations where this type of leader is a fit
- Pilot projects to test effectiveness
- Pilot evaluation to identify strategies for broader application
- Adjustments to appraisal, pay, and promotional practices

Stage 4

- Broad implementation of facilitative leaders
- Ongoing assessment and adjustment

Organizational Readiness Criteria

In order to be effective, facilitative leaders require settings where:

- Key players have a clear understanding of the nature of the facilitative leadership role and firmly believe that this role is critically important to the long-term success of the organization.
- Upper management can identify situations where facilitative leadership is a good fit.
- The upper management team understands and accepts that participative management may be a significant cultural change that will require a degree of adjustment and investment.
- Individual upper managers are willing to shift their personal style to one that is more collaborative and inclusive to send a congruent cultural message.
- The organization is prepared to increase empowerment to those teams that demonstrate their readiness for increased accountability.
- Upper managers accept that effective collaboration requires that they will periodically receive feedback from other parts of the organization.
- The organization is willing to simplify procedures and remove blocks that might slow progress or stifle creativity.
- Individual upper managers are willing to act as champions to teams to help them overcome barriers and access resources.
- Adequate funds have been made available to provide the training and development that facilitative leaders require.

- The organization has adjusted its leadership position descriptions to include the competencies of the facilitative leader to ensure that qualified people are hired.
- The criteria for evaluating leaders have been adjusted to reflect the competencies of the facilitative leader.
- The criteria for rewarding and promoting leaders have been adjusted to ensure that facilitative leaders are encouraged and respected.

Deploying these types of leaders requires both commitment and planning. A good starting point may be to assess organizational readiness using the above criteria to identify those areas that need further attention. To take this step, refer to the Organizational Readiness Assessment in Appendix A.

3

THE WORK OF THE FACILITATIVE LEADER

There isn't a single team in the world of sports that would consider taking to the playing field without a referee. Yet that's exactly what project teams do when they operate without a process leader.

Imagine a baseball game without an umpire to interpret the rules, make calls, and handle disputes. Picture a soccer game in which the referee periodically slips out of his or her neutral role to take a kick at the ball. These things don't happen in the world of sports because the vital role of neutral parties is universally recognized. Everyone knows that games would degenerate into undisciplined chaos without impartial oversight.

Now imagine a highly paid scientist who's heading up an important project yet periodically has to take time from his or her work to think about how to run a complex decision-making session or maintain the health of the team. Not only is this a major distraction, but unless that scientist is also a skilled facilitator, it's unlikely that he or she is aware of techniques for managing these interactions.

Unfortunately most organizations haven't fully realized that the underperformance of many of their most important initiatives is due to the absence

> No matrix team should operate without the support of a skilled process manager.

of skilled neutral parties. It's time that organizations recognized that neutral players are just as important to workplace teams as they are to sports teams.

Features of the Role

Facilitative leadership has several features that differentiate it from other approaches to leading. Some of these differences stem from what this type of leader does, and others are related to how he or she manages the work. Because these leaders are deliberately absent from content discussions and therefore don't direct members concerning the task, they are free to concentrate on managing the enabling structure.

Providing Structure

The first and most important role of the facilitative leader is to provide structure. Throughout their work, they make sure that all of the supporting mechanisms are in place; then they systematically manage them.

Masterful facilitative leaders are familiar with scores of structuring tools and use them consistently to ensure that all interactions are efficient and effective. These structuring tools fall into four major categories:

- Work management tools like project planning, work planning, budgeting, empowerment planning, and performance measurement
- Meeting management tools like meeting design, facilitation skills, and group decision-making methods
- Planning tools such as visioning, objective setting, gap analysis, environmental scanning, stakeholder analysis, and priority setting
- Problem-solving tools such as process mapping, action research, cause-and-effect analysis, survey development, systematic problem solving, solution generation, and action planning

Directive leaders may know many of these same processes, but facilitative leaders know how to apply each one in a team setting, as a neutral third party. For example, the directive leader may know how to write a vision statement and then communicate it to staff, but the facilitative leader knows how to design and run a participative visioning session in which team members collaborate to create a shared vision.

> Facilitative leaders know to apply processes in a participative manner.

Creating and Maintaining an Engaged Workforce

The second role of this type of leader is to create and maintain an engaged workforce, a focus area that has not been as important to traditional leaders. This can be accomplished in a number of ways:

- Building strong teams: Helping team members get to know each other and form close working relationships, clarifying empowerment, building agreements with and among team members, and creating teams norms that support positive interactions

- Maintaining team effectiveness: Implementing periodic evaluations of group effectiveness and other feedback activities, then making structured interventions to correct team problems

- Coaching individuals: Offering support to individuals who are in need of extra attention to improve their personal performance

- Coordinating training: Periodically assessing needs, arranging for training, coordinating field visits, facilitating debriefing sessions, and identifying mentoring opportunities

- Mediating conflicts: Providing third-party assistance to individuals and groups in conflict to restore effective working relationships

It's important to note that the tools that facilitative leaders use fall into two categories:

- Work structuring tools to help teams do their work—for example, process mapping, cause-and-effect analysis, and systematic problem solving
- Culture management tools to help team members improve relationships and increase team effectiveness—for example, team review, peer review, and leader feedback

> Facilitative leaders provide the structure that nurtures a collaborative culture.

Although all of these activities take place in meetings, facilitative leadership is far more than simply managing meetings. In a facilitative environment, a wide variety of meetings are held in order to accomplish specific results. That is, most of the meetings conducted by the process leader have nothing to do with regularly scheduled staff meetings.

The key processes that facilitative leaders use are described in greater detail in Chapter Four. What is important to note here is that facilitative leaders pay much more attention to the enabling structure than leaders in the past typically have.

Facilitating to Lead

The hallmark of facilitative leaders is how they use facilitation in their work. Many people are familiar with neutral outsiders who help make meetings effective. Although both meeting facilitators and facilitative leaders base their work on the same core practices and behaviors, they use very different applications:

Meeting Facilitators	Facilitative Leaders
Designed to be neutral outsiders	Designed to be neutral insiders
Use facilitation tools in meetings	Use facilitation tools in all of their work

Meeting Facilitators	Facilitative Leaders
Focus on meeting elements	Focus on the daily management of all functional elements, including meetings
Negotiate the power they need to manage meetings	Negotiate the power they need to manage all aspects of their work

Examples of how facilitative leaders use process tools to manage differently than traditional leaders do are set out in "Leadership Styles in Action" box (see end of chapter). You'll see there that each leader plays a very different role. The directive leader makes decisions, directs staff actions, and works with employees individually. In contrast, the facilitative leader provides process tools and then facilitates discussions so that members are supported as they take action.

When the directive leader makes decisions, he or she maintains a large measure of control. When a leader facilitates, he or she deliberately shares control so that member knowledge drives decisions and members are accountable.

While the job of the traditional leader is more difficult in many respects due to the emphasis on personal accountability, the job of the facilitative leader is certainly more interpersonally complex. Not only do these leaders have to perform the roles of trainer, coach, and mediator, but they also have the added challenge of creating the structures that enable employees to be effective.

> The main aim of the facilitative leader is to leverage the resources of group members.

The Seven Guiding Principles for Facilitative Leadership

The work of facilitative leaders is guided by a clear set of principles based in the core beliefs of facilitation: that people are intelligent and capable, want to do the right thing, and will take responsibility and assume accountability for their actions. These guiding principles form a mental model that informs every action taken.

Principle 1: Empowerment

Members are involved in managing all aspects of the operation at the highest possible empowerment levels. This creates high involvement and promotes self-management. The facilitative leader always asks:

"Who needs to be involved in this activity?"

"What's the highest empowerment level that's effective for this situation?"

Principle 2: Collaboration

Decisions are made in a way that synergistically blends differing ideas into courses of action that all parties can support. The use of consensus-building approaches strengthens commitment for key decisions and builds a cooperative culture.

The facilitative leader always asks:

"How can I involve people to incorporate their ideas?"

"What course of action represents a win for all parties?"

Principle 3: Creativity

Creative tension is injected to encourage members to question the status quo, be inventive, and explore new synergies. Risk taking and initiative are rewarded and new ideas championed and explored.

The facilitative leader always asks:

"What represents breakthrough thinking?"

"How can we make a quantum leap?"

Principle 4: Transparency

Relevant and important information is openly and honestly shared with team members and other stakeholders so that decisions are based on sound information. The work of the team is communicated in an open and forthright manner with those who need to be informed. The leader strives to create a climate in which people feel that they can express their honest opinions.

The facilitative leader always asks:

"What information do team members need to do their jobs effectively?"

"What information do we need to share with others?"

Principle 5: Systems Thinking

Actions are always taken within the context of the whole organization. Cause-and-effect thinking is employed to help people see the connections between their work and the work of others. Broader impacts are considered, and strategic alliances are made to form creative partnerships.

The facilitative leader always asks:

"What's going on elsewhere that connects directly to our work?"

"With whom do we need to connect and partner?"

Principle 6: Feedback

Feedback loops are built in everywhere to ensure that every aspect of both the operation and personal performance is continuously evaluated and improved. The team routinely debriefs its activities to identify lessons learned. Individuals periodically receive feedback about their performance to encourage personal growth.

The facilitative leader always asks:

"What did we do well? What could we do better?"

"How can each of us improve?"

Principle 7: Development

Learning and development activities are valued. Training and coaching are made available to each member to encourage personal growth. Teams engage in regular team-building activities to ensure their overall effectiveness.

The facilitative leader always asks:

"What skills and capabilities do we each need to develop?"

"What will make each of us more capable? What will improve the team?"

Applying the Guiding Principles

Facilitative leaders possess structuring tools that enable them to manage each of these guiding principles in a participative manner. Since collaboration is so important, they help members streamline their operations to find the time needed for these structured dialogues.

These leaders allow facilitative values and beliefs to guide all of their actions. They ask questions, clarify, and paraphrase, whether they're talking to one person in their office or to ten at a meeting. In every situation, they search for ways to engage, empower, and support the members of their team.

Facilitative leaders seek to develop the leadership talents of others: to instill confidence, authority, and responsibility in each person. The result of this approach is the creation of a culture that's collegial, collaborative, and self-managing.

The net effect of applying these principles is the creation of a collaborative workplace that engages its members, brings out the best ideas, and generates breakthrough results. In this environment, team members are more important than the leader. It's a workplace where the leader's main job is to help the members be great.

The Importance of Upward Feedback

Since facilitative leaders work for the members of their team, it is important that a regular upward feedback mechanism be put into place. This appraisal question-naire should describe the observable actions of the leader so that members can rate his or her performance based on their direct experience.

> Facilitative leaders aren't traditional leaders who periodically facilitate; they're facilitators who use process to lead.

The seven guiding princi-ples of the facilitative leader are reflected in an upward feedback instrument, the Facilitative Leader Index, that's provided in Chapter Seven. This questionnaire allows for direct observation and assessment of the extent to which the seven guiding principles are in effect.

A New Position Description

An important step toward acquiring and cultivating leaders who are capable of helping matrix teams achieve superior results is to create appropriate position descriptions. The following core competencies need to be incorporated into job descriptions for this role.

Facilitator
- Three to five years of experience as an active facilitator lead-ing a wide variety of discussions
- Able to design and implement essential processes that will enable groups to make collaborative decisions and coopera-tively manage their work

- Experienced at designing and running effective meetings
- Able to provide structure for large group interactions like planning retreats, public meetings, and forums
- Able to act as a neutral party in problem solving and planning discussions

Team Builder

- Experience as a team member
- Versed in the stages of team development and aware of which actions and interventions are needed at each stage to ensure that the team always operates at high performance levels
- Aware of the structured conversations that are important to building and maintaining positive interpersonal relationships

Project Manager

- Training in project management and experience as a member of a complex project team
- Knowledgeable about the steps of the project management process so as to be able to provide adequate structure to the group's work
- Able to manage goals, objectives, milestones, and expected results
- Able to provide stewardship to initiatives so that they remain on time and within budget

Continuous Improvement Expert

- Experience participating in a complex process improvement process
- Aware of the essential quality management tools used to find, analyze, and solve problems
- Able to help members map processes, gather and analyze data, name and solve problems, and identify improvement strategies that relate to both the task and the process elements

Trainer

- Familiar with the fundamental steps of planning and designing training activities
- Able to conduct training needs assessments, plan training sessions, and conduct short instructional sessions
- Capable of creating a learning environment where people share their experiences, try new approaches, and learn from each other

Network Builder

- An effective communicator who is skilled at locating resources, doing research, and passing on information to others
- Skilled at using technology to create a multidirectional flow of information

Coordinator

- Experienced in maintaining a network of resources and contacts
- Aware of the steps that teams need to take to create synergies and share resources with other groups

Coach

- Aware of the steps in giving detailed and timely performance feedback and improvement suggestions

Conflict Manager/Mediator

- Aware of the steps used to help individuals and teams resolve issues and mediate disputes
- Able to diagnose team dysfunctions and make structured interventions that restore team effectiveness

Of these roles, the most important is that of facilitator. This isn't only because the values of facilitation are at the heart of this management style, but these leaders continually and consistently

> Organizations need to create job descriptions for the role of facilitative leaders.

apply the guiding principles and core tools of facilitation in all aspects of their work. Whether they're dealing with a group or interacting with just one other person, they are always using active listening, questioning, paraphrasing, and summarizing to ensure effective communication. They also structure every conversation with others, whether it's with one person or thirty.

It's difficult to define exactly how skilled and experienced a person must be to be a highly effective process specialist, since this is such an individual practice. Some people are naturals and take to facilitation quickly, while others struggle for years to grasp the basics.

> Any leader who wishes to become a facilitative leader must first become a skilled facilitator.

Regardless of natural aptitude, it's safe to say that some formal training is essential and that three to five years of experience facilitating several different types of group sessions a week is required to be able to confidently manage the complex mix of process elements associated with most initiatives or departments.

This book does not aim to provide a primer about facilitation. Fortunately workshops and books on facilitation are readily available. To check your current level of competency as a facilitator, take the simple self-test provided in Appendix B.

The Supportive Behaviors

In addition to doing radically different work than traditional leaders do, facilitative leaders also behave differently. While traditional leaders are expected to be strong, assertive, and direct, facilitative leaders are unassuming, collaborative, and supportive. While traditional leaders stand in the forefront and receive more attention than their followers, facilitative leaders deliberately stand back and place their people in the limelight. Here are some of the behavioral guidelines that guide this style.

Be Positive and Energetic

In order to inspire creativity and innovation, these leaders exhibit enthusiasm for the work at hand. They talk about their commitment and help others to see what's possible. They keep up their personal energy to strengthen the vigor of the members. They maintain a can-do attitude even when facing difficult situations.

Be Neutral on the Task

Like all meeting facilitators, facilitative leaders stay neutral about the work of the group. They do not inject themselves into content matters or try to influence decision making. They are aware of how their body language might betray how they feel about various topics and guard their neutrality by using neutral language, responding with questions rather than answers, and deferring all content decisions to the members.

Be Firm on the Process

As a balance to remaining neutral about the content of the work, the facilitative leader is directive concerning the process elements. Structure is the domain of the facilitative leader, who is acting within the boundaries of the role to determine how things will operate. While the facilitative leader may choose to gain member input into process, he or she may also impose processes and monitor follow-through if it's in the interest of overall effectiveness.

Be Informed

Successful facilitative leaders gather extensive data about their members and the work of the group in order to fully understand the needs and dynamics of the situation. This understanding helps them ask the right questions, design the appropriate discussions, and select the tools that fit the situation.

Be Consensual

Facilitative leaders strive to help create outcomes that equally reflect the ideas of all members and that everyone can live with. They include stakeholders in decision-making discussions when they're likely to be affected by the outcome. They know how to reframe competitive decision-making discussions into collaborative ones that result in a win for all parties.

Be Unobtrusive

Facilitative leaders take a back seat to the members of their team. They do not compete with them for attention, but help showcase member accomplishments. They never try to be the center of attention or make themselves look important. They deliberately ensure that team members are in the forefront.

Be Flexible

Facilitative leaders plan ahead but also constantly monitor how things are unfolding so that they can adjust their processes to reflect changing realities. Their orientation is to be open to shifts in directions in order to be able to respond quickly. They adapt to changing circumstances rather than force members to take part in activities that no longer make sense.

Be Understanding

Facilitative leaders understand that there are great pressures in today's hectic workplace. These pressures sometimes cause people to exhibit antagonistic behaviors or fail to meet commitments. Rather than take a punitive approach to situations such as this, these leaders help people resolve their blocks and offer personal coaching.

Be Confident

Facilitative leaders never shy away from naming issues or surfacing problems. They proactively seek feedback from group members about their own personal performance and are prepared to act on improvement suggestions. Facilitative leaders always manage conflict in a forthright and assertive manner.

Be Optimistic

Facilitative leaders do not allow disinterest, antagonism, cynicism, or other negative emotions throw them off. They focus instead on what can be achieved and try to draw out the best from each participant. Whatever is happening in the group or to the project, the process leader maintains a can-do attitude.

The Importance of Assertiveness

Of the supportive behaviors, none is more misunderstood than the one related to being firm about the process. It's a common misconception that the facilitative leader's neutrality concerning the task renders him or her passive and unassertive. In reality, the opposite is true: effective facilitative leaders are just as assertive as traditional leaders. The difference is that they're assertive about different things. The directive leader asserts on the content, while the facilitative leader asserts on the process.

> The traditional leader tells employees, "Here's what I want you to do." The facilitative leader asks colleagues, "What do you need me to do?"

Facilitative leaders may not decide which product idea gets selected or which improvement plan gets implemented, but they do have a high level of control concerning how things get done. Here are just a few illustrations of that process assertiveness:

- Helping a group set measurable objectives and define outcomes, then monitoring time frames and feeding back

performance data so mem-
bers can deal with performance gaps

> Facilitative leaders man-
> age the process elements
> so assertively that they
> could not possibly be per-
> ceived as weak.

- Ensuring that group members adhere to the group
  norms that they have made a
  commitment to follow

- Ensuring that agreed-to decisions and procedures are being
  followed

- Managing time limits and topic boundaries at meetings

- Conducting reviews to ensure follow-through on implementation plans

- Helping team members evaluate their collective effectiveness
  in achieving their goals

- Implementing feedback activities that provide members with
  a detailed critique of their personal performance

- Creating feedback loops that ensure members objectively
  review activities to glean lessons learned

- Insisting that combative parties take part in a conflict
  mediation that they might wish to avoid

- Coaching individuals who are underperforming and then
  helping them monitor their performance improvements

Gaining Authority

Power is one of the central dilemmas of the role of the facilitative
leader because facilitation is intrinsically a powerless role. This
dilemma of powerlessness is also well known to all consultants, who
are used to operating without the traditional levers of power. But
facilitators and consultants aren't alone in this power vacuum. In
fact, more and more of today's leaders are finding themselves leading without real authority. This lack of authority has a number of
roots:

- Matrix teams are often composed of members who have been appointed by their respective departments or organizations, leaving the leader unable to hire, discipline, or fire them.
- The members of many teams have greater expertise, are more experienced, or have higher ranks than the designated leader.
- The job descriptions of some project managers are written in such a way as to limit them to roles like chairperson or coordinator.

The solution to this dilemma lies in knowing the power equation:

**The amount of power you have =
the amount of power you negotiate.**

This equation means that leaders who are operating in a power vacuum need to be constantly identifying the specific authority they require in order to be able to manage the process elements of their assignment. Then they need to negotiate to receive this power—not just once, but continuously throughout every stage of their work.

The first power negotiation should take place during the hiring phase to ensure that upper management is prepared to support them in exerting control over process elements. They will also need to negotiate authority levels during their first meetings with team members, upper managers, and other stakeholders. As the initiative unfolds, they will need to ask for additional power to manage specific situations.

Once power levels are agreed to, these agreements should be put in writing and added to the leader's position description. Here are a few examples of the specific powers that a facilitative leader might request:

During the Hiring Phase

- Acknowledgment of the unique role of this type of leader and commitment to evaluate that position using relevant criteria
- Commitment from upper managers to support reasonable requests for increased decision-making power for both the leader and the team

- Commitment to communicate fully and openly with the leader and the team
- Agreement that the facilitative leader's decisions regarding process elements will be respected
- Commitment of upper management to heed the facilitative leader's recommendations concerning staffing issues
- Commitment to support the leader when team members require coaching
- Commitment to abide by the recommendations emerging from any conflict mediations mediated by the leader

At the First Meeting with a New Team

- Agreement to abide by the process designs recommended by the leader
- Agreement from all team members that they will take part in creating behavioral guidelines and then honor them
- Commitment from team members to take part in team-building activities such as creating a team charter
- Commitment from all members to self-monitor their work schedule and work responsibly to achieve team outcomes
- Agreement from team members to take part in periodic team improvement activities such as routinely scheduled team and meeting surveys
- Commitment from all member to accept periodic 360-degree feedback
- Agreement from all members to accept coaching in the event of performance issues
- Commitment from all members to participate in any mediation activities prescribed by the leader

At the Start of Any Meeting Expected to Be Challenging

- Support of the process design created for the meeting rather than second-guessing or overturning it

- Commitment to take part in creating rules for the meeting and then to abide by those rules
- Acceptance that it is appropriate for the leader to facilitate assertively and make interventions whenever interactions become ineffective or if the meeting goes off track

During Any Meeting

- Agreement to abide by any interventions that are made to redirect behaviors
- Commitment to abide by the leader's decisions to end discussion, shift topics, or park items
- Adherence to the process steps within the meeting design

At the End of Any Meeting

- Support for the leader's efforts to bring closure to discussions and develop realistic action steps
- Commitment by members to assume responsibility for follow-through on all action items ratified by the members

It's important to note that even leaders who come fully equipped with officially sanctioned authority can end up powerless. We all know leaders who were given an official title and had clear authority to manage, but totally lost the followership of their people.

Facilitative leaders aren't fooled by either the illusion that they have power or the lack of officially sanctioned authority. They accept that leadership always depends on the consent of those being led. They know that if they're competent and skillful, team members will support them and grant them all the power they need. By extension, they also know that if they lack key process skills and aren't able to help their teams achieve important goals, there isn't an official job description in the world that can save them.

> Leaders who feel powerless have failed to negotiate the authority they need.

Leadership Styles in Action

Situation	Directive Approach	Facilitative Approach
Setting objectives for a new activity	Leader sets goals and communicates them.	Leader shares nonnegotiables and other parameters, then facilitates an objective-setting discussion.
Hiring a new team member	Leader sets criteria, interviews, and hires.	Leader helps members identify hiring criteria, then teaches interviewing skills so members can fill the vacancy.
Setting a budget	Leader sets the budget and communicates it.	Leader shares core budgeting skills, then helps group identify parameters they will use to set a budget.
Creating a work schedule	Leader creates a work schedule.	Leader helps members identify work scheduling guidelines, then facilitates schedule development discussions.
Choosing a new supplier	Leader chooses a new supplier.	Leader helps members identify key criteria for selecting a new supplier, then facilitates selection discussion.
Operational problem	Leader studies the situation to find solutions.	Leader asks members to study the situation, then facilitates a structured problem-solving discussion at which members identify solutions.

Leadership Styles in Action   *(Continued)*

Situation	Directive Approach	Facilitative Approach
Purchasing new equipment	Leader orders new equipment.	Leader helps members set up systems to assess equipment needs, then facilitates a discussion to review needs and select equipment.
Monitoring results	Leader assesses data and checks on subordinates.	Leader helps members set outcome measures and create self-monitoring mechanisms.
Staff under-performance	Leader conducts a performance review.	Leader coaches employee to overcome performance issues.
Infighting	Leader ignores it or talks to each individual.	Leader brings the two parties together to hear each other and look for solutions to end the dispute.
Poor execution	Leader identifies root causes and meets with individuals to discuss solutions.	Leader structures a debriefing session to identify what went wrong, then facilitates problem-solving discussions to find solutions for key mistakes.

4

TRANSITIONING INTO THE ROLE

Adopting a facilitative approach to leading is a complex change that requires varying degrees of accommodation depending on who is making the transition into the role. There appear to be three very different routes into the role:

- Leaders of existing groups may deliberately change their style by shifting out of directing content to focus on process in order to get staff to take charge. Leaders would do this in situations where the staff have already demonstrated that they are capable of managing the operation or to encourage staff to gain that capability.
- An organization may consciously hire a process-oriented leader to work with a team, project, or department. In the past, most leaders have typically been subject matter experts, but there is a growing trend to hire process experts, like professional project managers, to lead.
- A team of knowledge workers may be formed and then empowered to hire a facilitative leader to manage their processes so they're free to focus on their work.

Let's explore each of these situations in more depth.

When Existing Leaders Shift Their Style. This can occur in any traditional department or in any matrix team where the existing leader deliberately shifts from a directive style to a facilitative one in order to encourage staff to take on greater responsibility and accountability. In this situation, the leader abides by staff decisions as long as outcomes match expectations. If team members begin to underperform, the leader assesses the situation and either reassumes a directive style or applies remedies that will restore content control to members. These measures might include training, coaching individuals, removing impediments, and providing needed support.

Traditional leaders who shift to a facilitative mode often remain the content leader in selected aspects of the team's work while operating as the process leader in other areas. Leaders who possess highly developed skills in both content and process areas have greater versatility and can alternate between roles to match the needs of various situations. Leaders therefore can play both roles within the same group as long as they are always clear about what role they are playing and communicate that to team members.

> Directive leaders who don't master facilitation will stay stuck in the directive mode.

What makes leaders in this situation facilitative is not whether they're operating in the process mode 100 percent of the time but that they consistently use facilitative principles to guide their behaviors and actions.

When a Project, Department, or Team Is Assigned a Leader. This scenario can unfold in any department when the leader leaves or when a new project or initiative is launched. The tendency in the past has been to hire a specialist to serve as leader in the more traditional mode. This will continue to be effective in some circumstances, but unless leaders are expert in each of the specialties of their teammates, they will in fact be very limited as to the extent to which they can direct the work of members. If leaders in this situation also lack process skills, they will be left with little or nothing to do besides their own specialty work and trying to coordinate the efforts of colleagues.

It is for this reason that there's a growing trend toward hiring professional project managers to provide process expertise for complex initiatives. This is a step in the right direction but needs to go one step further.

Although project managers are process leaders, their tool kit is limited to processes that relate to managing project boundaries. Unfortunately, most still lack the group management and collaborative decision-making tools needed in facilitation. As a result of this skill gap, even experienced project managers may find that they know how

> Project managers need to add facilitation mastery to their repertoire to be truly effective.

to set goals but don't know how to gain member buy-in, or that they know how to set project milestones but don't know how to overcome resistance to a demanding timetable, or that they know how to clarify team parameters but don't know how to intervene at the team level if members become seriously dysfunctional.

Organizations that continue to hire leaders on the basis of their content knowledge need to ensure that these individuals receive facilitation training to enable them to be effective with specialists. When they hire professional project leaders, they need to assess the candidates carefully to ensure that their facilitation capabilities match their project management skills.

When a Team Hires Its Leader. This is an emerging trend in which a team of specialists is convened and then allowed to select their own leader to manage the process elements. The members identify the hiring criteria, interview candidates, and make the final selection.

Once process leaders have been chosen, they're given a clear contract that outlines their role and specifies how that role will interact with that of the content specialists. If the team also appoints a content leader, that role is clearly defined to ensure that it doesn't compete or overlap with the role of the facilitator.

The case of team members hiring their leaders epitomizes the essence of a total paradigm shift, since we have always assumed that staff worked for their leader, not the other way around.

> In the future, more leaders will be hired by their teams.

To illustrate the differences in the various roles that are in play in the typical project, consider the following sets of responsibilities (in situations where no single individual plays the content leader role, the process leader ensures that these responsibilities are assumed by the team members):

Responsibilities of the Project Sponsor (Upper Manager)

- Owns the business case
- Final arbiter of scope
- Sets overall direction
- Sets the tone
- Establishes objectives and targets
- Obtains commitment and funding
- Acts as communication link and champion
- Acts as intermediary
- Sets reporting format
- Is accountable to the management team for results

Responsibilities of the Senior Specialist (Content Leader)

- Maintains overall direction
- Provides subject matter expertise
- Ensures the right people are hired
- Marshals needed resources
- Helps to schedule activities
- Negotiates empowerment with upper management
- Takes part in the work of the team
- Identifies when course correction is needed

- Represents the team at specialist meetings
- Monitors progress
- Meets with the senior specialist to discuss progress
- Adjusts the work schedule
- Helps evaluate results

Responsibilities of the Facilitative Leader
(Process Leader)

- Is in charge of the process
- Meets with key players to understand the project
- Facilitates creation of a detailed process map for the initiative
- Designs detailed process agendas for each meeting held by the team
- Assertively facilitates all group discussions
- Provides team members with training in group skills
- Conducts team-building sessions
- Helps the team negotiate empowerment
- Monitors process effectiveness
- Plans and makes needed interventions
- Helps members document and publish minutes
- Proposes and designs needed processes
- Helps the team evaluate outcomes

Questions and Answers About the Role of Facilitative Leader

What is the ideal situation for a facilitative leader?

The best situation is to be hired as a neutral outsider by a team of self-managing specialists under a clear contract to manage all of the process elements with the committed support of each member and of the organization.

If leaders don't set direction or make substantive decisions, are they really leading?

This very much depends on what you call leading. If leading is telling people what to do, then facilitative leadership is not leading. But if you define leadership as creating the conditions for outstanding performance and fostering leadership in others, then this person is definitely a leader.

When a facilitative leader creates an effective enabling structure and assertively manages the boundaries, the mechanics, and interactions, members will feel well led.

If there's a senior content expert on the team, then isn't that person the leader?

There are teams that need both a content leader and a process leader. Since these two roles are very different, it isn't difficult to differentiate them and have the leaders work cooperatively. In these situations, the content leader has the final word concerning the work of the team, and the process leader exerts control over enabling mechanisms. If areas of responsibility are well defined, these roles should mesh and support each other rather than clash.

Can a person hired by team members really assume the leadership role?

Conventional thinking would say that this isn't possible, but new paradigm thinking recognizes that leadership is gained, not bestowed. We all know of authoritative leaders who lost the support of their people despite having the title and official authority levels.

In the same way, a facilitative leader who is trustworthy and effective at helping the team achieve its goals will gain the team's support. By negotiating to obtain specific powers, any leader can gain the leverage needed to operate effectively.

Can an established leader become a facilitative leader?

Even very directive leaders can shift their approach if they learn to facilitate and then implement training and coaching activities that encourage their people to become capable of taking charge.

The main barrier to changing leadership styles without moving to a new setting is established mind-sets of both upper managers and staff.

Upper managers are often reluctant to make the changes that are needed to support this type of leadership. It is also common for staff to resist changes that will increase their personal accountability and autonomy levels.

Leaders in this situation need to orient both upper managers and staff to the changes they're making and gain their buy-in to the shift. Strategies to gain staff support to this shift are provided on page 28. The section on organizational readiness on page 32 will also provide fuel for conversations that lead to greater understanding.

Leaders may want to take a gradual approach to shifting their approach. They can begin by demonstrating facilitation skills in meetings, then encourage their staff to also gain these skills and share responsibility for meeting management.

One of the most significant tools in shifting leadership styles is the Four-Level Empowerment Grid in Chapter Two. When empowerment levels are slowly and gradually adjusted as the capabilities of staff increase, the transition to a more participative workplace can be systematically staged.

Can a leader play both the content and process roles?

Although it is easier to define the boundaries of the role if the facilitative leader is a neutral outsider who has no vested interest in the decisions made by the group, this isn't always possible. Often leaders who have expertise related to the task will be adding the role of facilitator to their repertoire. When this happens, they will need to balance the demands of these two roles carefully. Here are some of the strategies leaders in this situation can use:

- Leaders who expect to play both roles need to explain these two functions and identify when each will be used.
- Leaders should identify the topics where they will retain the

content expert role and the amount of decision-making authority they will be exerting in each of their specialty areas.

- At the start of each decision-making discussion, leaders should clarify the specific empowerment level for that topic to avoid misunderstandings about the intent of engaging members. Team members always need to know if they are being asked for their opinion as input to a decision that will be made by someone else (level II), if they're making a recommendation that needs approval (level III), or if they are making a decision that has been fully delegated to them to make (level IV).

- Expert leaders who are facilitating need to guard their neutrality by avoiding the use of overly leading questions and taking care not to praise some ideas but not others. Members will see these slips as attempts to use facilitation to manipulate them and will no longer trust the leader in that role.

- If the leader needs to be part of a conversation and there is no one else to act as facilitator, the leader can wear one hat for the opening section of the meeting when they are laying out the process, then switch hats for the discussion. In these instances, facilitator roles like writing on the flip chart and keeping track of time can be distributed among the members. That way attention is still being paid to process, but the group is not deprived of the full participation of the leader.

- An expert leader who also facilitates must consistently honor member decisions in order to build trust in his or her neutrality.

Playing both roles is not impossible, but it takes planning. Leaders who are the content expert in a particular subject should not remove themselves from that discussion and deprive the group of their wisdom. Similarly, process is so important to group effectiveness that leaders should always provide it, even when they're also going to play the content leader role. Realistically, most leaders can expect that they are going to find themselves alternately wearing both hats.

When should leaders not facilitate?

Leaders should not take on this role if:

- They don't understand the role and have few process skills.
- It distracts them too much from their other work to also play the facilitator role.
- Their content expertise is so great that it would be ineffective for them to be neutral in most discussions.
- Their temperament is a poor match for the behaviors needed to facilitate well.

If a team is unable to hire a neutral outsider and the leader shouldn't take on the role, another strategy is to arrange for facilitator training for the entire team and then rotate the role among members. Then everyone will understand the function and be supportive of each other as they take turns.

Are there situations in which this type of leadership should not be used?

Facilitative leaders should not be deployed in situations where employees are unable to work independently and where the organization doesn't intend to empower. These are usually situations in which workers are inexperienced or jobs are unskilled. These situations benefit more from the clear direction and daily oversight provided by a directive leader.

How do I become a facilitative leader if my organization is unaware of the need for this type of leader and doesn't actively support it?

Until awareness about the nature and importance of facilitative leadership is more widespread, these types of situations will be common. An important first step is to gather information about this role and share it with key thought leaders. Pioneering facilitative leaders may consider identifying some strategic allies within their organization such as the head of human resources or a specific upper manager and ask that person to act as their sponsor while they implement this change.

The strategies for overcoming resistance to process outlined on page 26 may be helpful. Facilitative leaders can also gain leverage from continuously monitoring the impact of their work and periodically reporting the results of various evaluations to their upper management to further overcome their resistance.

The Challenge for Employees

When leaders facilitate and organizations empower more, employees are also required to undergo a transformation. How much they need to adjust will depend on their circumstances. There will be little or no adjustment required for knowledge workers who are already self-directed and fully accountable. These workers will not want to work with a leader who oversees their work or delegates tasks. Facilitative leadership is a natural match for their needs and capabilities. But workers accustomed to operating in a traditional top-down setting often find the shift to working with a facilitative leader to be a significant challenge.

Employees in hierarchical organizations are seldom well informed. Sometimes even middle managers aren't consulted about strategic issues and have little decision-making authority. In these settings, frontline employees are supervised and expected to be compliant. Over time these workers may have become conditioned to be both dependent and subservient.

The word historically used to describe a worker in this state is *subordinate*. The dictionary definition of subordinate is, "of lower rank or class; a dependent; subject to the control of another; a junior person; an underling; one who is inferior." This notion of inferior beings doing what they're told to do is largely a remnant of the industrial era, which was characterized by assembly lines staffed with unskilled workers performing fragmented tasks. Although these kinds of workplaces continue to exist, their numbers are dwindling, particularly in industrialized nations.

These types of working conditions are not only disappearing in large technology-based companies; they're even becoming a thing of the past in factories where assembly line workers are now working in teams and commonly take part in complex process improvement efforts.

Despite the transformation of work, there are still many subservient-minded employees in the workplace. Because of this, facilitative leaders should not be surprised if they find themselves assigned to groups that aren't used to making substantive decisions and whose members are reluctant to assume increased responsibility.

While one would assume that all workers want to be consulted and to manage their own work, there are lots of people who want simple, well-defined jobs. These employees expect their leaders to make the substantive decisions and provide explicit direction.

This state of dependence may have any number of sources. Employees may feel unsure of their own abilities or be concerned about how they'll look to their colleagues if they start making suggestions at meetings. Or they may simply not want to be held accountable for outcomes.

Whatever the cause of this outlook, these staff need a comprehensive orientation to the concept of participative management as well as assurances from upper management

> Employee buy-in is critically important.

that they will not be punished for taking risks or speaking out. Deploying the buy-in strategies outlined in Chapter Two will be helpful when introducing this concept to staff. Once these steps have been taken, employees need to either buy in to the concept of working in a participative culture or relocate to positions that will continue to operate with more traditional jobs.

Employees as Partners

In order for a facilitative leader to be effective, all team members must see themselves as full and valued partners in the enterprise. Consider the definition of partner: "An ally; an associate; a colleague. People working together in the pursuit of a common goal. Equal roles in a shared activity." When employees are partners, they:

- Participate in goal setting rather than wait for the goal to be handed down to them.
- Set personal objectives, then plan and control their own daily activities.
- Take full responsibility for getting their jobs done to high standards that they help set.
- Monitor their own progress and report on results achieved.
- Take the initiative to find and fix problems and improve work processes.
- Exchange feedback about personal performance with their peers.
- Participate on teams and take part in team-building activities.
- Assume major responsibility for their own training and development.
- Share skills and expertise with colleagues.
- Continuously seek ways of innovating and adding value to their team and to the overall organization.
- Develop their own facilitation skills and use those skills to help lead their team.

Rights of Partners

Once employees have shifted their frame of reference to that of partner, it's important to balance this by granting the rights of partnership:

- To be told the mission and business strategies of the organization
- To have access to important organizational information

- To be treated with consideration and courtesy
- To have their professional opinion listened to and respected
- To be consulted, particularly concerning matters that affect them personally
- To operate in a climate free of fear and reprisal
- To be in direct contact with internal customers and colleagues
- To maximize their personal potential through training and development
- To be creative, take risks, and try new ideas
- To develop and exercise personal leadership

Responsibilities of Partners

The rights of partnership are balanced with a new set of responsibilities that are designed to ensure that both the leader and the organization receive the support they need. All partners in a participative workplace must understand that they will be expected to:

- Extend a trusting and positive attitude toward leaders and the organization.
- Create a set of personal goals and results indicators that mesh with the goals of the organization.
- Demonstrate competence and commitment in achieving those goals.
- Work responsibly without supervision to self-manage activities.
- Accept increased empowerment and responsibility levels.
- Help the team to make improvements in processes and products.
- Share information, especially about problems, so that preventive action can be taken.
- Give and receive feedback about performance.

- Responsibly coordinate roles with others so that there is a fair and balanced workload for all team members.
- Act like a team player, placing "we" before "I."
- Refrain from interpersonal fighting, seeking solutions instead through dialogue and mediation.

When employees embrace the rights and responsibilities of partnership, the stage is set for the facilitative leader to create a workplace that supports growth and innovation.

Peer Feedback

Ultimately the effectiveness of any team is determined by the extent to which members are accountable to each other. In the facilitative organization, it isn't only that the leader is now accountable to the members, but that members are also accountable to each other. To reinforce this concept of mutuality, it's important for members to regularly give each other detailed feedback based on observable, behaviorally based criteria.

A sample peer evaluation feedback instrument, the Empowered Partner Index, has been included in Chapter Seven. This instrument is intended to be completed by teammates, but may also be filled out by anyone else who has detailed information about the performance of a member, such as support staff, upper managers, customers, the leader, and other stakeholders.

Peer feedback is an indispensable tool for fostering mutual accountability.

Once a questionnaire has been developed and administered, results can be shared at a survey feedback meeting, such as the one described in Chapter Six. A modified version of the needs and offers process can also be used, in which team members take turns meeting one on one to share needs and make personal offers that will enhance their working relationship.

Setting aside several hours every six months to give and receive peer feedback represents a major change from the past. Careful attention will need to be paid to the issues of confidentiality and trust to ensure that team members feel safe enough to offer their colleagues honest assessments.

Once teams become accustomed to this activity, its tremendous value will become readily apparent. The power of lateral feedback is that it not only reinforces the core concept of mutual accountability but provides valuable data for personal performance improvement. Lateral feedback is often taken far more seriously than top-down appraisals since colleagues value the insights and approval of their peers. Lateral reviews are also an avenue for conflict resolution when individuals correct low-rated items that might have led to conflicts further down the road.

5

MEETING MASTERY

While facilitative leaders use their team members and process skills to inform their actions outside meetings, they are also masters of meeting effectiveness. This is important since meetings are proliferating in workplaces and are a major source of wasted time. Although this book is not a comprehensive resource for running effective meetings, there are a few key points about meetings that need to be made here, since facilitative leaders manage them differently than traditional supervisors or managers do. This variance stems from the fact that teams convene meetings for different purposes than traditional work groups do.

People who work in a traditional department typically come together at weekly staff meetings to get direction, share information, make a few joint decisions about issues that affect other members, and coordinate the relatively few activities that overlap their separate roles.

Members of a team need to get a lot more out of meetings due to the interconnected nature of their work. They need to get to know each other, learn to be a team, formulate a common goal, build their collaboration skills, identify objectives and milestones, create joint action plans, and then agree on roles and responsibilities. Once an initiative is under way, teams use their meetings to track progress on achieving joint objectives, exchange feedback about each other's performance, give feedback to the leader about his or her performance, and improve the effectiveness of the team as a whole.

Since so much collaboration goes on in matrix networks, it is imperative that every meeting be carefully structured and efficient.

Doing More at Meetings	
How Traditional Work Groups Use Meetings	*How Teams Use Meetings*
Get direction	Build relationships
Share information	Share information
Make decisions	Learn team skills
Update each other	Set goals and objectives
Coordinate roles	Plan and coordinate work
	Manage empowerment
	Monitor progress
	Find and solve problems
	Identify lessons learned
	Give and receive feedback
	Improve the team and its meetings
	Evaluate results achieved

This means that the days of simply getting together once or twice a week to read a few memos and bounce around an idea or two are gone. Given that so much needs to get done at meetings, it is imperative that each one be carefully structured and skillfully facilitated.

Unproductive meetings are not an option for teams.

The importance of effective meetings can't be overstated. It doesn't matter if all of the members of a team are individually brilliant; if they can't make an effective group decision or create synergies, the overall success of their efforts may well be in jeopardy.

Four Types of Conversations

Four distinct types of conversations can take place in facilitator-led meetings:

- *Information-sharing sessions* include sharing news and recent developments, presentation of reports, and reviewing progress.

Since these types of sessions are not aimed at making decisions, they do not require major attention to process and are chaired rather than facilitated.

- *Planning sessions* address activities such as visioning and creating goal statements, describing objectives and output measures, assessing needs, identifying priorities, and creating detailed action steps. Budget planning and program planning meetings fall into this category, as do design sessions. Managed-change initiatives are also planning activities. Because decisions are made during planning conversations, they require considerable attention to process and need to be actively facilitated.

- *Problem-solving sessions* involve participants in identifying and resolving issues. The core activities are gathering data, identifying problems, analyzing the current situation, identifying potential solutions, sorting solutions, and planning for action. Customer service initiatives and process improvement projects feature a large number of these types of conversations. Since decisions are made in these types of discussions, problem solving needs to be carefully structured and systematically facilitated.

- *Relationship-building sessions* encompass all conversations aimed at building cohesion and shared commitment such as norm development discussions, feedback and coaching sessions, and all conflict mediations. A team-building workshop is an example of a relationship-building session. Traditional groups rarely engage in these types of discussions, but teams must have them in order to build and maintain effective working relationships. Since important agreements are made during relationship-building discussions, they also require attention to structure and active facilitation.

Most meetings are a blend of these types of conversations. In some cases, a single meeting may have a mix—for example, one-third information sharing, one-third planning, and one-third problem solving. The Sample Blended Agenda shows a single meeting with such a blend; the agenda assumes there are eight members and two hours for the meeting.

Sample Blended Agenda

Agenda Item	*Process Notes*
1. Agenda overview: 10 minutes	*Purpose: To clarify and ratify the purpose and outcome of the meeting.* • Leader reviews objectives and time allocation for each item, makes changes, and ratifies refined agenda.
2. Progress updates (information sharing): 45 minutes	*Purpose: To share important news about work in progress.* • Roundtable briefing by each member to update colleagues on recent progress and to report on items brought forward from previous meetings.
3. Focus group design (planning): 30 minutes	*Purpose: To create a detailed process design for upcoming customer focus groups.* • Review purpose and scope of activity. • Post four information categories on walls: current customer needs, customer's pressures, trends and innovations, customer's wish list. • Members move from chart to chart, confer with colleagues, then record potential questions. • Total group reviews suggested questions. • Multivoting to prioritize suggested questions. • Referred ranked lists to focus group subgroup for final focus session question selection.

Sample Blended Agenda *(Continued)*	
Agenda Item	*Process Notes*
4. Resolving the customer contact problem (problem solving): 25 minutes	*Purpose: To identify and rank the problems with the current customer contact system.* • Staff present data concerning facts of the current customer contact system. • Force-field analysis is used to identify what's working and what's not. • Multivoting of nonworking elements to rank blocks and barriers. • Refer ranked issues to the customer service improvement sub-group for problem solving.
5. Agenda building: 10 minutes	*Purpose: To begin the agenda-building process for the next meeting.* • Parked items are reviewed and considered for inclusion. • Multivoting is used to identify importance and time requirements for each item. • Members complete the exit survey as they leave to generate data about meeting quality. • Adjourn.

Facilitative leaders always know which types of discussions they're leading.

Most often, separate sessions are held for each type of conversation. A team may, for example, hold a weekly information sharing meeting, then schedule periodic planning, problem-solving, or team-building sessions as the need for each arises. This ensures that adequate time and attention are paid to each type of discussion.

Beyond Regular Staff Meetings

Since teamwork demands so many meetings, it's important that leaders know how to design and facilitate dozens of different special-purpose meetings. Here is a compendium of some of the ways that meetings can become faster and more efficient and how traditional staff meetings can be reinvented.

Information-Sharing Sessions

Standing Check-In or Daily Huddle

What is it? A fifteen-minute update session in which only the most essential information is shared and no one sits down. Can act as an *anti-meeting* if it eliminates the need for a longer meeting

When to use it. To share the latest news and updates quickly and efficiently or as a team huddle at the beginning of the day or shift.

How does it work? A timer is set, and in a round-robin format, members share the latest information that they feel others need to know. Key points are recorded on a flip chart. People can ask questions, but there is no debating or deep exploration. Items that require more in-depth discussion are referred to a future meeting. The fifteen-minute time frame is firm.

Personal Blitz

What is it? A regularly scheduled fifteen-minute session with the leader and an individual team member to talk one-on-one about progress, problems, issues, and news. Conducted in person or by telephone.

When to use it. Once a week with each team member to ensure that every team member has direct contact with the leader.

How does it work? A standard time is scheduled for the updates. The team member reports first. The leader also reports and responds to as many questions as possible. Follow-on actions are agreed to.

Twelve-Minute Briefing

What is it? A fast, to-the-point management briefing by the person on the team who knows the most about the subject in question.

When to use it. To avoid preparing long, detailed briefing notes on minor points. To avoid involving a lot of extra people who are not needed to answer a straightforward question.

How does it work? When upper management needs information, the expert in that subject requests permission to do a short presentation instead of preparing a lengthy report. He or she invites upper management to submit specific questions they wish to have answered. A face-to-face meeting or teleconference is then scheduled with the expert and management representatives to share technical and factual information.

Town Hall

What is it? A briefing with upper management or key stakeholders to update them on progress and get their on-the-spot approval to take action. A forum for gaining management commitment and participation.

When to use it. When you want to accelerate movement on a project and need to get key players on board quickly.

How does it work? Team members prepare briefing notes. Leaders and stakeholders are invited to a one- to two-hour session. Seats are arranged in a circle in a large room to encourage dialogue. Team members make recommendations. After each recommendation, the facilitator asks for comments and advice. After each discussion, approval is sought to proceed, and an upper manager in attendance is asked to become the champion for that initiative.

Participative Keynote

What is it? A way of sharing information in a participative forum.

When to use it. When you want to hear from an expert but fear rambling, drawn-out discourse. It can also be used as an alternative to the usual way the head of the organization addresses a large staff meeting.

How does it work? Participants sit in small groups at tables instead of theater style. They spend fifteen to twenty minutes in discussion and come up with questions that they want the speaker for the session to address. They write these on cards, which they turn in to the speaker, who sorts them during a break. The speaker then makes his or her presentation with special emphasis on answering the participants' questions. As an alternative, you can post the key questions on the intranet a week in advance of the session to identify the questions that participants wish to have addressed.

Planning Sessions

Future Quest

What is it? A tool to build a shared vision of the future in a large group. A large group gathering of thirty to sixty key players who are asked to jointly create a picture of the ideal future.

When to use it. As the starting point for strategic planning efforts. Whenever you want to get a large group of people to play an active role in a major change effort.

How does it work? Meet in a large room with empty walls on which to post sheets of paper, each with a question about the current situation. These questions can address topics like the state of the economy, the environment, trends, current success stories, competitor profiles, needs of key players, strengths, opportunities, and obstacles. Place seats in a circle in the middle of the room. Have a keynote speech by one or more stakeholders to set the context. Then allow time for participants to talk with others and record their responses to the posted questions. When all sheets are full, hold a plenary session to share all of the ideas. Multivoting can then be used to identify the most important elements in each area. Ideas are collected and passed to the strategic planning core group.

Remote Poll

What is it? A quick way to use technology to gather information from a panel of experts in advance of a planning session.

When to use it. When experts are geographically dispersed or too busy to attend a meeting.

How does it work? Once the focus of the planning activity has been clarified, identify the subject matter authorities whose opinions are sought and solicit their involvement. With their help, create six to eight specific questions to which they will respond. Questionnaires typically feature open-ended questions but can include closed-ended questions as well. Use the Internet to send the questionnaire and retrieve responses. Circulate responses to the participants in advance of the planning event.

Innovation Fair

What is it? A session to share news about innovations as a starting point for a conversation about creating synergies between products and services and spark creative ideas.

When to use it. To create breakthrough thinking by tapping into the collective intelligence of a large group.

How does it work? Invite a wide cross-section of people to start collecting ideas about their favorite products or services. These should be people from outside the system who can lend a fresh perspective: customers, students, suppliers, retirees, artists, even children. Encourage them to bring pictures, or draw or build a representation of what they consider to be innovative. This can be an existing thing or a theoretical idea. Find a large room to showcase the items, and ask the participants to talk about what makes them great. Record the key concepts that make these ideas innovative. Next, create small groups to hold creative brainstorming sessions to find ways that current products or services can be inspired by the ideas presented. Share the ideas, and use multivoting to identify the best concepts.

Problem-Solving Sessions

Focus Group

What is it? A session held to test a new idea or get a reaction to a single idea or proposal.

When to use it. When you want to test ideas for new approaches that would have an impact on employees, suppliers, or partners.

How does it work? The idea or proposal is explained to a group of four to eight stakeholders. The process could be as simple as inviting stakeholders to identify the pros and cons of the proposed idea. They could also be asked to describe the potential impacts of the idea if it were to be implemented.

Workout

What is it? A large group problem-solving session in which twenty-five to sixty stakeholders identify strategies to overcome problems and enhance the effectiveness of a selected product, process, or service.

When to use it. When it's desirable to change a major system, product, or service quickly. When you want to benefit from the ideas of all stakeholders and get their active participation in the implementation stage.

How does it work? A product, process, or service is selected for improvement. Data are collected about the existing situation. Key stakeholders are identified and invited to take part. Data are then shared with the stakeholders in advance of the session. A large room is arranged theater style for a kick-off briefing by upper managers and key stakeholder representatives. The managers then leave, and groups of six to eight participants adjourn to separate breakout rooms to discuss what's working and what's not working about the current situation. The nonworking items are prioritized to identify the top-ranked ones.

The small groups reconvene and present from three to six of their top-ranked items. These are recorded, duplicates are eliminated, and a multivote is held with the entire group to identify the top six to ten blocks and barriers. The top issues are then posted on walls, and members sort themselves into small teams to work on specific items. Groups adjourn for several hours to analyze their specific issue and then brainstorm solutions. They sort their solutions on an impact-effort grid and prepare proposed action steps to implement the top-ranked suggestions. A town hall meeting is then held to share the recommendations with decision makers, who can offer advice and then give on-the-spot approval to proceed. Managers are asked to serve as champions for initiatives to ensure that they don't encounter bureaucratic blocks.

After-Action Debriefing

What is it? An assessment conducted after a project or major activity to determine what happened and why. It compares intended behaviors and results with actual behaviors and results. It seeks to discover what to keep doing and what to change.

When to use it. To glean lessons learned. To understand what made something work so that successes can be duplicated. To avoid a repeat performance if major mistakes have been made.

How does it work? Key players meet to review the event and recap how each individual activity played out. The original goals and objectives of the activity are reviewed to provide a benchmark for the debriefing. The facilitator then poses a set of questions to elicit information about what worked, what didn't work, why certain actions were taken, how players reacted to them, why corrections where not taken on the spot, what assumptions people made, and what resources and supports helped and hindered. To conclude, group members create a summary of lessons learned.

Relationship-Building Sessions

Intergroup Mediation

What is it? A structured meeting between two parties with an unresolved dispute that's blocking cooperation and needs to be resolved.

When to use it. When a dispute arises that is not resolving itself and is hampering overall effectiveness.

How does it work? Get both parties to agree to take part in a mediation. Create safety norms to set a supportive and safe climate. Find a large, private room and set aside one to two hours. Ask each party to its overview of the situation or

grievance. Ask the members of the other party to listen neu-
trally and take notes. Reverse roles and repeat the process.
Send each party to a separate breakout room to write up a
summary of what the other group said. Invite the groups
back to present their summaries. If the summaries are accurate, separate the groups again to write up a list of what they
need from the other group in order to settle the dispute.
Groups reconvene to share their needs lists and answer
questions. They then go back to their separate breakout
rooms with each other's needs list and discuss offers that
they are prepared to make to end the dispute. Groups reconvene to share their offers. If the offers are accepted, the
meeting ends. The offer lists are typed and distributed. In six
to eight weeks, the offers are turned into surveys and circulated to members. Members are brought together to identify
strategies to ensure all offers are honored.

Feedback Rounds

What is it? A structured feedback meeting at which everyone
on the team both gives and receives feedback from others.

When to use it. Periodically to help members understand how
they are doing and to share helpful tips.

How does it work? Create an atmosphere where people feel safe
giving and receiving feedback by facilitating a discussion to
create safety norms. Seat members in a circle around a large
table. Hand out a sheet of paper to each person on which
each writes his or her name. Ask each person to pass his or
her sheet to the person on the right. As sheets go around,
each team member writes comments to teammates in
response to two topics: "What you're doing that's effective;
keep on doing it" and "What you could do to be even more
effective." When every member has written on every sheet,
team members are given a few minutes to read and reflect on
their feedback.

The sheets are sent around the table again, and this time each person reads aloud his or her positive feedback. This is called a *strength bombardment*. The last activity is to go around the table and invite each team member to share one or two personal change commitments based on the improvement suggestions received in the exercise.

Facilitating Teleconferences

One of the major meeting trends in every workplace is that more and more meetings are happening at a distance. Although facilitation was created for face-to-face meetings, there are a number of key elements that can be borrowed from the facilitator tool kit to help make distance meetings more effective.

First, consider some of the special challenges of meetings conducted over the telephone:

- People can't see each other, so these meetings tend to feel impersonal and disconnected.
- Interaction is stilted because people can't see each other, so conversations tend toward one-way information sharing.
- Since people have to wait for a chance to talk, teleconferences can drag on for far too long.
- Sometimes people sit in silence for long stretches listening to conversations that have nothing to do with them.
- It's impossible to read body language to pick up on the nonverbal clues that identify how people are feeling or whether they're fully engaged.
- If differences of opinion crop up, it's difficult to manage the conflict effectively, bring other people into the conversation, or help the parties arrive at a mutually agreeable solution.
- Although minutes are usually sent out afterward, no flip chart notes are taken during conversations to keep everyone focused and help the conversation move forward.

- Teleconference participants could be doing any number of distracting things during the session: reading, eating, working on their computers, or sorting out their desks.
- It's easy for people to walk in and out of a teleconference without anyone noticing.
- If materials weren't sent out ahead of time, it's harder to hand out new information.

Because they are naturally difficult to manage, teleconference sessions need to be actively facilitated. The facilitation techniques that most improve them are many of the same ones that work in a face-to-face meeting: providing a clear purpose, describing the process, conducting a warm-up exercise, encouraging interaction, making interventions, conducting periodic process checks, paraphrasing key ideas, offering periodic summaries, and ensuring that key items have closure and clear action steps. Here is how you can use these strategies to improve any telephone conference:

Before the Teleconference

- Contact participants by telephone or e-mail to seek their comments on the agenda.
- Create a detailed agenda with process notes that identify the various types of conversations that will be held (information sharing, planning, problem solving, relationship building).
- Identify who needs to be involved and for which segments of the call, plus the information that each player needs to prepare. Avoid involving more people than absolutely necessary.
- Distribute the agenda to the participants so they can do their homework and dial in to the call at the time they'll be needed.
- Set a time limit for each call so people know what to expect.

At the Start of the Teleconference

- Conduct a roll call to establish that people are engaged and ready to proceed. If applicable, ask each person to state what he or she needs to get out of the meeting. Record these personal goals, and refer to them throughout the meeting to help keep people engaged and let them know you have them in mind.

- Create a name map on a blank sheet of paper in front of you.
- Beside each name, write down the person's stated goal for the session. As the meeting progresses, make a check mark beside people's names every time they speak. This will remind you of who is on the line and what they need to get from the session. It will also help you identify the people who need to be brought into the conversation.
- Review the agenda to clarify the overall purpose of the call, the purpose and process for individual segments, and time associated with each segment. Also be clear about who needs to be part of which conversations.
- Clarify the rules of teleconferencing. This can be a facilitated conversation or you can propose a core set of teleconference norms (see the box) in advance of the call and ask participants to amend and ratify it.

Proposed Teleconference Norms

To ensure that this call is productive, we will all:

- Make a commitment to be attentive to the conversation and avoid multitasking
- State our names before starting to speak
- Be as clear and concise as possible
- Ask for clarification if it's needed
- Freely express concerns and opinions
- Speak up if we notice we've been silent for too long or if a particular conversation needs to wrap up
- Engage others by asking questions and offering opinions
- Strive to stay focused
- Ask for a summary if we need to get refocused
- Announce if we are leaving the call

During the Teleconference

- At the start of each topic, review the purpose, process, and time frame for each item.
- Call on people by name both to present and to comment on what others have said. Keep track of who is getting airtime.
- Periodically make process checks to ensure that things are still on track. Ask questions like the following:

  "Is the purpose still clear?"

  "Is our approach working?"

  "Are we making progress?"

  "Is the pace okay? Too fast? Too slow?"

  "Have we lost anyone?"

  "Do we need to move on?"

- To bring closure to a topic, offer a summary of the key points that were made. If it was a decision-making discussion, turn the summary into a decision statement. Then conduct a roll call and ask each person to accept the final decision.
- Help the group create action plans for any topics that need them. Encourage people to take responsibility for follow-through.

At the End of the Teleconference

- Review the summaries for each topic and the action steps that have been identified.
- Invite each person to say whether his or her goal for the meeting has been achieved or to make a statement of what he or she got out of the meeting.
- Conduct a brief evaluation by asking people to identify what worked, what didn't work, and ideas to improve future teleconferences. If this is impractical, create an evaluation form online, and e-mail it.
- Share details about when and how the minutes will be distributed.

- Identify the date and time of any future teleconferences.
- Express thanks for everyone's participation, and sign off.

Although teleconferences are inferior to face-to-face meetings, they are a fact of life. If anything, there will be more of them in the future rather than fewer. Because they are proliferating it's important to structure them and ensure that they are run just as efficiently as any other meeting.

Preventing Meeting Problems

Since meetings are naturally prone to becoming problematic, facilitative leaders should preemptively engage members in a discussion about meeting parameters early in the life of any initiative.

Because buy-in is always greater when the members themselves suggest rules, the facilitative leader's first strategy is to ask targeted norming questions that will prompt members to suggest norms similar to the ones below. If members don't come up with the rules that are needed, it is acceptable for the leader to suggest these guidelines for ratification by members.

Most meetings will be made significantly better if the following rules are in effect:

- All meetings will be run with a clear goal and expected outcome; no meetings will be held for the sake of having a meeting.
- All meetings will be run with a clear process design to guide discussion; there will be no unstructured thrashing about.
- Everyone will do their homework and come prepared to make decisions.
- Everyone will come to meetings that they have made a commitment to attend.
- Everyone will arrive on time and stay for the duration.
- Distractions such as working on laptops or talking on cell phones will be strictly avoided.

- Where possible, all meetings will be segmented, with people required to attend only the sections that pertain to them.
- Information sharing will be accomplished as much as possible outside meetings to cut down on time spent doing updates.
- When action plans are created, they will be brought forward at a future meeting to ensure follow-thorough.
- Everyone will be time sensitive and voluntarily limit their participation to avoid dominating.
- The designated facilitator will have the support of all members and may intervene if necessary to maintain focus.

> Special rules or norms can help prevent common meeting problems.

Monitoring Meeting Quality

Regardless of the preventive measures taken, maintaining meeting quality requires periodic improvement efforts. Conducting these types of reviews is one of the hallmarks of facilitative leaders. Old-style directive leaders never tune up their meetings; facilitative leaders do it all the time. This tune-up involves using brief exit surveys on a regular basis and implementing a formal meeting effectiveness survey and survey feedback discussion at least twice a year.

Meeting effectiveness surveys are not included in this book since they are readily available in dozens of books on meeting management and group effectiveness. Refer to the Further Reading section for a list of suggested books on meetings and group facilitation. The survey feedback process useful for analyzing the results of any survey is described in Chapter Six.

Spending time to assess and improve meeting quality may seem like a waste of time to many people, so it's important to remember that nothing else wastes precious time as much as badly planned and poorly run meetings.

> Effective meetings are a key feature of all facilitative organizations.

The bottom line is that ineffective meetings are not an option and should never be tolerated. Taking a few hours every six months to conduct and debrief a survey about current meetings can serve only to save time in the long run.

6

THE TEN
ESSENTIAL PROCESSES

The defining feature of facilitative leaders is that they offer process and structure rather than directions and answers. In every situation, they know how to design discussions that enable group members to find their own answers.

This chapter explores some of these essential core processes. It does not detail every process design that leaders need to know, since that would take hundreds of pages and repeat material already well documented in scores of excellent books on core management topics such as strategic planning, project management, and total quality.

Among the processes I do not describe are those that are already well known and relate to achieving the task, such as goal setting, creating measurable objectives, establishing milestones, budgeting, process mapping, and communication planning. Also not repeated are many of the fundamental facilitation tools, such as systematic problem solving and brainstorming, that all experienced facilitators already know and use.

The processes that I do detail are those that are still relatively underused and relate to managing relationships and building a collaborative culture. These are the processes that are unique to the facilitative approach to leading: new leader integration, visioning, team launch, operational review, survey feedback, after-action debriefing, needs and offers negotiation, peer review, interpersonal conflict mediation, and coaching.

Matching Processes to Stages

While many processes are intended for ongoing use, others are applicable only at specific stages in the life cycle of a team or project. At the start of a new initiative, leaders will be designing and facilitating a lot of planning activities that provide a strong foundation for the independent action of staff—for example:

- Conducting planning meetings at which group members review parameters, clarify their vision, set measurable objectives, identify milestones, create action plans, negotiate appropriate empowerment levels, create a detailed communications plan, and agree on reporting mechanisms

- Leading team start-up discussions in which members get to know each other, identify personal skills, set group norms, clarify roles and responsibilities, reach agreement about how to work as a team, and produce a team charter document

- Identifying learning gaps and coordinating training sessions, field trips, and benchmarking initiatives that help members gather the information they need

- Negotiating a contract that defines the role of the facilitator, reporting relationships, and the areas within and outside of the leader's control

Once a project or team has begun its work, facilitative leaders spend more time designing and leading activities aimed at maintaining maximum efficiency:

- Managing regular staff meetings, which includes getting input into the agendas, creating meeting process designs, facilitating discussions, and distributing minutes

- Conducting periodic learning needs assessments and coordinating training and development activities that meet the emerging learning needs of the members

- Leading after-action debriefing to glean lessons learned
- Leading problem-solving sessions to help members analyze external blocks and barriers to progress and identify solutions
- Implementing periodic survey feedback activities to assess the effectiveness of the team, the meetings, and the overall project and then helping members create action plans for improvement
- Implementing feedback loops that allow members to safely exchange performance feedback with each other and with the leader
- Coaching individuals who are experiencing performance problems
- Mediating conflicts that exist between individuals on the team or between the team and other groups
- Holding meetings that help the members monitor follow-through on action plans

Toward the end of a project or work cycle, facilitative leaders help members bring closure in these ways:

- Helping the team evaluate its final product and wrap up its work
- Implementing personal performance appraisal processes
- Presiding over meetings such as town hall sessions to share outcomes with upper management and stakeholder groups
- Helping members celebrate successes and adjourn.

The Processes

The structured dialogues that are described in this section are hallmark activities that distinguish this leadership approach from all others. While some directive leaders may be familiar with and even use some of these same processes, only facilitative leaders systematically apply them as a cornerstone of their work.

Each of the processes described is most effective when conducted as face-to-face meetings. Given the realities of geography, however, it may be necessary to conduct parts, or even all, of some of these processes from a distance if this represents the only way that some of them can be used.

When planning distance dialogues, it is important to remember that personal conversations like team building, new leader integration, and conflict mediation are much less effective when participants aren't in the same room.

> The essential processes are integral to the methodology of the facilitative leader.

Essential Process 1: New Leader Integration

Facilitative leaders understand that the bonds of allegiance never form because of official announcements and that staff always need to buy in to their leader. To accelerate integration, they conduct a structured dialogue between themselves and group members in the first few days of the relationship to break down barriers and accelerate bonding.

What Is It? This process is a dialogue designed to establish a relationship between any group and its newly appointed leader. It is also a communication process that allows people to share information and get to know each other and an ideal opportunity for leaders to orient staff to their leadership style and for the parties to reach agreement about how they will relate.

What's the Purpose? The dialogue seeks to relieve anxieties and smooth the transition to a new leader, develop familiarity and trust, provide an opportunity for staff to accept their new leader, and create a forum for negotiating roles and power levels.

When to Use It. Use this process whenever a new leader joins a new team. With appropriate adaptations, this process can also be used to integrate a new individual into the team or to introduce two teams to each other.

What Are the Activities and Steps? This process begins with a meeting between the new leader and the team:

1. A preliminary meeting is held at which the new leader introduces himself or herself, makes a brief presentation about being optimistic for a shared future, and then invites members to take part in the new leader dialogue process.

2. The leader asks group members to hold a short meeting without him or her present to create a group profile based on questions such as these:

- Who are we individually? (education, expertise, family, hobbies)
- Who are we as a team? (our mission, objectives, products or services)
- Who are our stakeholders? What do we owe each one?
- What are our goals over the next six months, year, three years?
- What are we currently doing well?
- What are our proudest accomplishments to date?
- What aren't we doing well? What's blocking us from being effective?
- What words describe the state of our group, team, or department?
- What leadership style works best for us? Why?
- What do we most need from a leader in order to be effective?

3. While the staff are working on their responses to create a profile of the group, the leader answers a similar set of questions:

- Who am I? (education, work history, expertise, family, hobbies)
- My personal goals for the next six months, year, three years.
- My personal strengths and proudest accomplishments.
- My personal weaknesses and blocks to being truly effective.
- The words that describe my approach to leading.
- What I most need from my team in order to be effective. [This is the point at which the leader introduces the generic powers that he or she needs the members ratify. Refer to Chapter Three for examples of the authority that facilitative leaders typically seek from team members.]

4. At the integration meeting, team members take turns sharing their personal profiles and then present the responses to the group questions. Once members have completed their presentation, the leader presents his or her personal profile. Throughout the presentations, anyone may ask clarifying questions. Parties can also ask the other to accept specific points.

5. At the end of the session, notes are circulated to all members.

What's the Outcome? Group members and the new leader learn a great deal about each other quickly. Many operating guidelines are established. The session also affords the group an opportunity to identify what they need from the new leader and for the leader to ratify the general powers he or she needs in order to operate effectively.

On the contextual level, this process is a significant strategy for initiating a major paradigm shift. The mere act of initiating this conversation sends staff a message that this is an interactive and responsive leader and that a new culture of partnership has been established. It establishes mutual accountability and demonstrates the style of the new leader effectively.

Essential Process 2: Visioning

Since process leaders don't determine the direction or desired outcome of their teams, it is essential that they possess a collaborative process that will help group members define the end state. Visioning is a key activity that results in alignment around a shared goal.

Visioning is most useful at the start of any team or initiative to help members build a collective picture of the desired future, but it has many other uses. In fact, skilled facilitators use visioning all the time as a goal-setting tool. A set of visioning questions can be asked at the start of a day-long planning session, a one-hour problem-solving meeting, a career-planning discussion with a single team members, or a conflict mediation.

What Is It? This is a participative approach to goal setting that engages group members in describing a picture of the desired future.

What's the Purpose? The purposes are to engage people in planning their own future, encourage creative visualization of what's possible, and ensure that everyone engaged in the initiative shares the same view of the desired outcome.

When to Use It. This process can be used at the start of any new team or new initiative or at the start of any meeting or new relationship. It is also an ideal participative technique for large strategic planning meetings since it can be conducted with any number of participants.

What Are the Activities and Steps? In this process, the leader and the team together consider the future:

1. The leader clarifies the parameters, assumptions, and non-negotiables relevant to the situation. He or she then asks members to imagine that it's the end of the activity. If it's a one-hour meeting, members are asked to imagine that they are leaving the

meeting. If it's a project, they are asked to imagine that it is three to five years in the future and that the activity has been successfully completed. The leader then poses five or six detailed questions to channel member thoughts. These questions draw out the important details of the desired future. Members are given several minutes to write their responses. Visioning questions are always created to fit each situation. The box illustrates a sequence of visioning questions for a new project.

Example of Visioning Questions for a Project

Imagine that it's exactly three years from today, and we're here to wrap up our work and celebrate this team's great success!

- Describe the specific improvements we've made.
- What new programs, innovations, or cutting-edge ideas did we create?
- What major problems or blocks did we overcome?
- What's special about how we're serving our customers?
- What's our most amazing achievement?

---

2. When each person has had an opportunity to respond privately to the questions, invite members to find a partner to take turns hearing each other's vision. Ask partners to scatter around the room to add privacy. People can sit or stand. Allocate two to four minutes for the first partner to share his or her vision. Ask the other partner to listen actively. When the time is up, the partners switch roles so the second person can share his or her vision.

3. Ask each person to find a second partner and repeat the dialogues. Repeat as many times as desired. In small groups, it's often advantageous to repeat the activity until all team members have spoken to each other. The more dialogues that are held, the more people gain insight into each other's idea.

4. Once members have returned to their seats, facilitate a discussion to pull the ideas together. You will find that ideas have

already become somewhat homogenized through the partner conversations. The synthesizing process can be done by testing collaboration on each point or recording all ideas and then using multivoting to rank the main points to identify the defining features of the group's desired future. The notes from the session are typed and circulated to members.

What's the Outcome?   Visioning generates a detailed depiction of the future that helps create alignment. Since group members participated in the activity, they have a sense of buy-in and are more likely to work hard to realize the vision.

At the midway point of any activity, the key points of the vision can be used as the basis for a survey that asks members to rate the extent to which the initiative is making satisfactory progress. This reminds members that their criteria are being used to drive the work of the team.

Essential Process 3: Team Launch

Complex matrix projects demand a high degree of cooperation and collaboration. Members need to get to know each other, understand each other's skills, create clear ground rules, align themselves around a common goal, and clarify exactly who's doing which part of the assignment.

Groups that jump into their work without taking the time to establish a solid foundation run the risk of ending up as a fractured group that's forever unable to evolve into a cohesive and effective team. Building capable teams is so important to the success of most matrix activities that all facilitative leaders are experts at both building and maintaining them.

What Is It?   This is a set of conversations that provide the members of a new team with clear parameters and the opportunity to develop cooperative relationships.

What's the Purpose? The conversations help team members get to know each other, define working relationships, establish the culture of the team, and provide a clear framework for the operation.

When to Use It. Team launch is used when a new team is formed or to relaunch an existing team that has experienced a significant change in membership or operating conditions. Specific launch elements may need to be revisited periodically through the life of a lengthy project.

What Are the Activities and Steps? In a series of discussions facilitated by the team leader, the new members:

1. Share information about their personal backgrounds, education, work experience, and special skills.
2. Review the key parameters of their project or initiative, such as the budget, time frames, and organizational expectations.
3. Engage in visioning to create a clear picture of the desired future.
4. Develop a set of specific objectives with results indicators that describe expected outcomes.
5. Create a set of norms or team guidelines that define how members will govern themselves.
6. Clarify the specific roles and responsibilities of team members as they relate to specific activities and objectives.
7. Help create an empowerment plan that describes decision-making authority for individuals and for specific activities.
8. Reach agreement on the specific roles, powers, and responsibilities of the process leader.
9. Create a communication plan that identifies how the team will communicate internally and externally.
10. Plan when and how the team will run its meetings.

What's the Outcome? These ten conversations provide an opportunity for members to get to know each other and build a foundation for their working relationship. The discussions also allow the leader to establish his or her position within the team and foster the creation of norms that build a collaborative and trusting environment.

After thorough team start-up discussions, a team will be able to create a team charter that documents the parameters of the team and helps those outside the team understand its work.

Essential Process 4: Operational Review

Another of the defining activities of the facilitative leader is the routine use of systematic problem solving to overhaul the team's operation periodically. While many leaders and teams are familiar with the steps of systematic problem solving, most use it in the context of process improvement efforts, where it is a core activity. Facilitative leaders, in contrast, use problem solving to identify and remove operational blocks to ensure that their projects don't become stalled.

What Is It? This is a structured conversation aimed at evaluating the process elements of an initiative rather than the task. It starts with an identification of what's working and what's not working to ensure that blocks and barriers are identified and removed. Then it engages members in systematically resolving blocks and barriers.

What's the Purpose? The purposes are to ensure that blocks and barriers are properly identified and then eliminated and that the work of the team is not hindered by organizational or operational factors.

When to Use It. This process can be used after the team or project has been operating for long enough to have encountered blocks and barriers, at the midpoint, and at least once every six months in a multiyear project.

What Are the Activities and Steps?   Here the team works together to ensure that the initiative is effective:

1. Team members are asked to monitor the effectiveness of the overall operation. A special meeting is scheduled when all members can attend. In the first structured discussion, staff identify all of the things that are working well and are helping the team achieve its outcomes. These positive elements are recorded on a flip chart sheet.

2. Group members are then asked to identify all of the hindering factors. These are the blocks, barriers, and obstacles that are getting in the way of the team's achieving expected results. (In some initiatives, it may be necessary to map operational processes or do other data gathering to be able to create an accurate picture of constraints.) This list can also include things that are missing or lacking. However, it does not include interpersonal relations or the performance of individuals, which are dealt with using personal feedback processes.

3. Multivoting is used to rank all of the constraining factors to identify which items most need to be addressed. Once blocks and barriers have been prioritized, systematic problem-solving sessions are scheduled to address each issue. If time allows, one or more blocks can be tackled at the operational review. Otherwise a schedule is created to begin holding problem-solving meetings to address specific issues. While some of the problem-solving sessions will need to be attended by the entire group, many problems can be tackled by subgroups.

4. The process applied during these sessions is the multistep systematic problem-solving model familiar to all skilled facilitators. Action plans are ratified by the entire group, and progress is reported back to the large group at regular team meetings.

What's the Outcome?   Blocks and barriers are routinely eliminated to ensure they don't derail the work of the project or department. Members are engaged in finding and solving problems to tap into their knowledge of the operations and reinforce their ownership.

Essential Process 5: Survey Feedback

One of the most used process tools in the facilitator tool kit is survey feedback. This involves administering a survey and then sharing the data with team members or other stakeholders who identify solutions for the low-rated items.

This process is in constant use because it can be applied to improve any aspect of an operation that is underperforming. As with the operation review, the key to this activity is that problems don't land on the leader's desk but are addressed by team members and stakeholders.

What Is It? This is a process of generating data using a survey and then providing those data to stakeholders for interpretation and identification of action plans.

What's the Purpose? Survey feedback is used to tune up the operation by engaging members or stakeholders in assessing the current situation, as well as identifying solutions.

When to Use It. This process is used to assess the effectiveness of any part of an operation and identify improvement strategies.

What Are the Activities and Steps? Team members engage in a number of steps and activities to review the initiative:

1. The area to be addressed is identified, and a survey is designed. This survey can be about meeting effectiveness, team effectiveness, product quality, process efficiency, customer satisfaction, leader effectiveness, or employee satisfaction.

2. The survey is circulated and completed anonymously. Completed surveys are returned to a delegated group member for tabulation.

3. The tabulated survey results are shared with the members at a survey feedback meeting. The first discussion held is to review all of the items that received high scores and list the reasons for these positive ratings.

4. The low-rated items are addressed as well. If only a few items received low ratings and the group size is small, the entire group can take part in a discussion to explore the reasons for the low ratings and then find solutions. If there are a high number of negatively rated items, a multivote may be needed to sort the items into batches to identify those that are most in need of attention.

In some settings, trust levels may be too low to discuss negative issues openly. In these cases, the low-rated items can be posted on the walls where clusters of group members confer with colleagues to answer two questions: "Why did this item receive a low rating?" and "What can be done to improve this rating?"

5. When the solution generation step is complete, use multi-voting again to identify the best improvement ideas for each issue. Hold a plenary session to share top-rated improvement ideas and form subgroups to create action plans for each issue. Ensure that action plans include monitoring and evaluation mechanisms. Circulate a report of the results and ensure that there is a process to report on implementation of improvements.

What's the Outcome? All aspects of the operation are routinely reviewed and improved. Members and other stakeholders are fully engaged in improving the operation of their organization. Frustrations about operational inefficiencies are not allowed to linger.

Essential Process 6: After-Action Debriefing

The most innovative and adaptive organizations are those that continuously learn from both their successes and mistakes. The facilitative leader schedules conversations to debrief all major activities to glean lessons and further enhance the operation.

Most after-action debriefings are conducted by those who managed the activity or event, but customers and other stakeholders can also be engaged in helping the organization debrief the effectiveness of an event. Having staff facilitate after-action reviews with focus groups of their customers before attending a session where staff go through the same process can provide fine insights.

What Is It? This is an assessment conducted after a project or major activity to determine what happened and why. It compares intended behaviors and results with actual behaviors and results and seeks to discover what to keep doing and what to change.

What's the Purpose? This process assesses the efficiency, effectiveness, and quality of an event in order to learn lessons for future application.

When to Use It. This can be used after any activity to understand what made something work so that successes can be duplicated and avoid a repeat performance if major mistakes have been made.

What Are the Activities and Steps? The assessment is carried out through the group process:

1. Key players meet prior to the event or activity to identify the specific goal and measurable outcomes. They also describe the characteristics of the implementation process and the desired impacts on other stakeholders.

2. After the activity has been conducted, key players meet to review the details of the event. The facilitator asks the group to compare the actual activity with the goals and outcomes identified in advance. The facilitator also asks questions to elicit information about what worked, what didn't work, why certain actions were taken, how players reacted to them, why corrections were not made on the spot, what assumptions people made, and what resources and supports helped and hindered. While face-to-face after-action debriefings are ideal to benefit from the synergistic interaction of group members, some benefit can be derived from conducting these types of assessments using the Internet.

3. When the assessment is complete, help group members create a summary of lessons.

What's the Outcome? The team members benefit from their own and the others' insights and learn lessons that will enhance the operation. The debriefing process shifts the culture from one where blame is ascribed to one where learning is prized. Once again this process reinforces that team members are accountable and responsible for all aspects of the operation.

Essential Process 7: Needs and Offers Negotiation

This is the most powerful process for managing relations between a leader and team members. It's a particularly valuable tool in view of the fact that the facilitative leader is often operating without real authority. This tool allows both the members and the leader to ask for what they need to make their relationship more effective. In this way, it provides a mechanism for both parties to adjust their roles and enlarge their powers.

Need and offers negotiation is an invaluable tool for resolving disputes between any two parties. These disputes can be about roles, style, behaviors, or a past occurrence that caused a rift. You will see that needs and offers negotiation is part of the process for mediating conflicts as the tool that brings closure to the session.

What Is It? This is a constructive dialogue between two parties to resolve misunderstandings and identify action steps both can take to create an effective working relationship. The process can be applied to improve relations between a leader and staff or to normalize relations between any two parties in a dispute.

What's the Purpose? This is used to generate safe, constructive feedback, identify action steps to remedy a relationship issue, and establish mutual accountability between parties. It can be used as a periodically scheduled conversation to fine-tune any relationship.

When to Use It. Although needs and offers negotiation can be used at the start of a new relationship to establish agreements about how the parties will work together, it is most effective once parties have been together long enough to know each other's working style. It is an essential conversation to resolve issues between two people or two parties. The facilitator can also use it in any meeting to gain acceptance of his or her needs from participants.

What Are the Activities and Steps?   Constructive dialogue begins with a safe environment:

1. The leader creates a safe environment by asking participants to identify the conditions that need to be in place for them to be able to give and receive feedback. These safety norms are recorded and posted.

2. Parties are separated to encourage openness and anonymity. Each party discusses what he or she needs from the other party in order to be effective. While gripes and concerns may be expressed, these are not recorded. All negative comments are rephrased as needs, written in the form of constructive and doable requests. For example, a negative complaint like, "You micromanage us," gets expressed instead as, "We need to report in writing once a week rather than daily."

3. The parties come together and take turns reading each other their list of needs. Listeners are advised to adopt a neutral demeanor. Questions of clarification are allowed, but no one may refute a need expressed by the other party. Defensive comments are also discouraged.

4. Parties trade needs lists and adjourn to their separate rooms. This time each party identifies what he or she is willing to offer the other party in response to that person's stated needs. Each party may also offer things that are not in response to a needs request.

5. The parties come back together and take turns sharing their offers. If one or both parties are not satisfied with the other's offers, repeat the previous step. The negotiation session ends when both parties have accepted the other's offers.

6. All of the offers are typed and circulated. Each party is expected to live up to the agreements made during the session. Within a reasonable period (ranging from weeks to several months),

the leader turns each set of offers into a short survey for rating by the other party. The ratings that are received will identify which offers have been honored and which items still need work.

7. The leader conducts a survey feedback meeting to review the high-rated items and look for suggestions about what can be done to improve the ratings of any low-rated items.

What's the Outcome? Both parties gain insight into what they could do differently. Relationships are mended, and positive feelings are restored through the act of listening nondefensively and then responding to expressed needs. Issues and misunderstanding are corrected when parties act on the offers that they have made. Group members learn that they have a safe and effective outlet for their issues with their leader.

Needs and offers negotiation is an invaluable tool that should be repeated at least every six months during a multiyear relationship to ensure that relationship issues don't build up without resolution. This dialogue also allows a team to mature since it provides members with an avenue to periodically request greater autonomy and increased empowerment.

Essential Process 8: Peer Feedback

Colleagues who work with any matrix team are accountable to each other. If one person fails to do his or her work, teammates may need to take up the slack. And if an individual is incompetent or irresponsible, the entire enterprise could be placed in jeopardy.

To be congruent with that principle, collaborative organizations need to replace traditional top-down performance appraisals with peer review. This is especially the case when the leader has insufficient content knowledge to be able to assess the work of staff.

Making team members accountable to each other is a major change but worth doing. Once colleagues have become accustomed to it, they will recognize the great benefit of peer input to their personal and professional growth.

What Is It? This is a mechanism through which members can give and receive feedback and a form of intervention when feedback is directed to individuals who are underperforming.

What's the Purpose? This process provides members with valuable performance feedback using a mechanism through which group members can surface concerns and constructively suggest improvements to each other. It reinforces the concept that group members are accountable to each other and thereby strengthens the team.

When to Use It. Peer feedback can be used at regular periods, say, at six-month intervals, once group members have been together long enough to know each other's work habits. It can also be used to resolve member disagreements.

What Are the Activities or Steps?
Peer feedback begins with the leader and members working together:

1. The leader asks members to identify the elements of personal performance about which they would like to give each other feedback—for example, "meets deadlines," "willingly helps others," "behaves in a professional manner," "works within professional standards," and "communicates effectively."

2. The leader creates a peer feedback form that features the selected criteria in a grid, along with the names of the team members. The survey is circulated to group members so that they can anonymously rate the performance of their colleagues. Each person rates all of the group members, including himself or herself.

3. The completed forms are returned unsigned to a predetermined administrator for tabulation. This person collates all of the ratings and shreds the originals. In each tabulation, one high and one low score is discarded in each column to reduce the influence of biased self-rating.

4. Group members receive only a copy of their ratings results. At a subsequent staff meeting, each person is asked to share his or her highly rated items and also to make at least three personal change commitment statements to address the lower-rated items. No one is asked to disclose their scores or which items received low ratings.

To create safety, but also enhance accountability, consider revealing results only to respondents during the first round of peer feedback, then documenting results in the team member's personnel file, in addition to sharing the results with the leader.

What's the Outcome? Team members receive valuable input from their colleagues. They also feel accountable to each other and take responsibility for personal performance improvement. The leader is given information that may be useful to coach underperformers. The team is given a constructive mechanism for dealing with people who are letting down the team.

Essential Process 9: Mediating Interpersonal Conflict

Whenever people work together, the potential for disagreement is present. While traditional organizations tend to avoid dealing with conflict, facilitative organizations constantly name their problems and seek solutions.

As soon as an interpersonal conflict occurs with a matrix team, the leader brings the two parties together to discuss the dispute and resolve it. Under no circumstances does the leader talk to the individuals alone or take responsibility for resolving the issue for them. Instead he or she offers the parties a set of steps that lets people safely vent their feelings and find their own solutions.

What Is It? This is a safe technique that helps parties in a dispute resolve their differences and rebuild their relationship.

What's the Purpose? This process makes the parties in a conflict responsible for finding solutions that end their dispute and resolving conflicts before they affect the entire team.

THE TEN ESSENTIAL PROCESSES   113

When to Use It. It can be used in situations where there is a conflict between two individuals and the members seem unable to resolve it themselves.

What Are the Activities or Steps? These steps enable team members to resolve disagreements:

1. The leader approaches each of the parties in a conflict to inform them that he or she will be mediating their disagreement. A convenient time is set and a private place is secured for the intervention.

2. If there is resistance to taking part in the mediation, the leader can ask each member to identify the conditions that would make him or her feel both confident in the outcome and safe enough to take part. (People typically state that they require conditions such as privacy, confidentiality, being spoken to in a respectful manner, and assurance that the other person will take the proceedings seriously.) Combine the conditions requested by both individuals, and circulate these to both parties as the parameters for the meeting.

3. When the parties arrive, they are seated to face the leader and advised not to speak to each other. The leader reviews and ratifies the conditions they developed in step 1, and reads a set of posted rules aloud:

- Each person will have an uninterrupted opportunity to present his or her views.
- The other person will listen without making random comments, displaying negative body language, or refuting any points.
- The person who is listening must make notes to summarize what the other person is saying.
- The listener may not refute, argue, or present his or her views.
- Anyone can ask for a short break.
- Dialogue ends when both parties are satisfied with the outcome.

- The facilitator is in charge and can make any needed interventions.
- Only the facilitator can end the session or dismiss the participants.

4. Ask the first person to share his or her view of the situation. The listener must act neutral, make eye contact, and write down the key points made by the other person.

5. When the first speaker is done, ask the listener to read back a summary of what he or she heard. Check with the other person to determine if this summary is accurate and acceptable. Stay with the first speaker until that person feels satisfied that he or she has been fully understood.

6. Repeat this process with the second person. Once both parties indicate that they feel that they have been heard, ask them to go to separate rooms for a period to reflect in private and make notes about what they need from the other person in order to be able to move forward and end the dispute. (Some parties may need to adjourn overnight.)

7. When the parties come back together, have them take turns sharing their needs. Again insist on nondefensive listening and allow clarifying questions.

8. Have the parties exchange their list of needs. Separate them again to allow them to reflect on the needs expressed by the other person. Ask them to come back with offers that correspond to those needs.

9. Facilitate a dialogue in which parties make offers to each other. Keep fine-tuning the offers until both parties are satisfied that they have solutions they can live with. Record these commitments, and set a specific time and date to return and evaluate the extent that each offer has been satisfied.

What's the Outcome? Responsibility for resolving disputes is placed on the shoulders of those involved. Specific plans are created to reestablish effective working relationships. Everyone on the team knows that conflicts will always be dealt with immediately in this respectful yet effective manner.

Ultimately this process can save a team from self-destructing over infighting, jealousies, and other interpersonal pitfalls. The basic steps of this process can easily be adapted to settle disputes between groups.

Essential Process 10: Coaching

Individuals can let down their team just as easily in a high-technology setting as on the shop floor. There are myriad reasons why people underperform. Unless the reason is poor physical and mental health, these people need to be encouraged to raise their level of performance.

Poor performance is often noticed by colleagues first and can therefore be most effectively identified using a peer review process. If peer feedback, additional training, and removing obvious blocks fail to produce the desired results, coaching is an important next step.

Facilitative leaders are at somewhat of a disadvantage when coaching knowledge workers if the underperformance relates to task elements such as whether the individual is working to professional standards or has the skills to perform the function. In these cases, the leader may need to ask a peer or a specialist outside the team to coach the individual.

Although the facilitative leader is not in a position to critique the expertise of the person, he or she can nonetheless offer coaching support for the work performance aspects such as timeliness, communication, and relations with others. The leader can also encourage the member to identify strategies for enhancing their professional expertise.

What Is It? This is a series of discussions during which the person being coached receives helpful feedback and is supported in identifying personal improvement strategies.

What's the Purpose? The purpose is to support positive, personal change and respond to the problem of individuals who are letting down the rest of the team.

When to Use It. The main time to use this process is when a staff member has been identified as underperforming. It can also be used as a developmental tool to help effective individuals who are performing well reach higher goals.

What Are the Activities or Steps? Coaching is accomplished when the facilitator and person being coached work together:

1. After the need for coaching becomes apparent, the coach begins to maintain detailed records about the specifics of the employee's performance problem in order to be able to offer performance feedback.

2. The recipient of the coaching is given information about the scope of the coaching activity in order to gather data about his or her performance.

3. At the first session, the coach sets a positive and optimistic tone for the process and then describes the general area of concern. The person being coached is given an opportunity to share his or her perception of how he or she is performing. This response allows the coach to assess the team member's level of self-awareness about the problem and openness to change.

4. The coach asks the person being coached to listen nondefensively to specific feedback about his or her performance, which is shared in a factual, specific manner. The feedback is always detailed and descriptive, never personal or critical. For each feedback point, the person being coached is also told about the specific impact of his or her actions on others.

5. If resistance and denial surface, these feelings are acknowledged but not allowed to distract from the need for the person to accept the facts of the situation. In tough cases, people can be

allowed some time to absorb and reflect on the information in private.

6. The person being coached is asked to identify specific and detailed action steps that will address underperformance. This encourages the person to take responsibility for making improvements. The leader then offers suggestions, building on the team member's ideas wherever possible.

7. The person who is being coached is asked to prepare a written personal improvement plan that is detailed and specifies outcome measures and time frames. The leader offers assistance in helping the person achieve his or her goals.

8. Sessions are scheduled to follow up on actions. Coaching sessions continue until performance improves or the effort is deemed to be of no use.

What's the Outcome? Underperformers are encouraged to take responsibility for creating a personal performance improvement plan that includes targeted outcomes, action steps, and follow-up activities with the leader.

Scheduling the Essential Processes

The activities described in this chapter are important to facilitative leadership. When they are used properly, they add to the health and effectiveness of any enterprise.

There is a danger, however, of overloading the already busy schedule of any team or project with process conversations. It is therefore important to space these discussions so as not to overload people's timetables or spend too much time on these types of activities within any one month.

One strategy is to plan an annual calendar of these activities so that staff can plan accordingly. With the exception of visioning, after-action debriefing, coaching, and conflict mediations, which are scheduled when specific needs arise, the rest can be scheduled.

A Sample Schedule for the Essential Processes is an example of a calendar and shows proposed spacing of the processes. Of course, these sessions need to be balanced with all of the other meetings that members need to hold in order to manage the work of the group.

A SAMPLE SCHEDULE FOR THE ESSENTIAL PROCESSES

Month 1	Month 2	Month 3
Process 1: New Leader Integration	Process 3: Team Launch	Process 5: Survey Feedback on meeting quality
Month 4	Month 5	Month 6
	Process 7: Needs and Offers Negotiation	
Month 7	Month 8	Month 9
Process 4: Operational Review		Process 8: Peer Feedback
Month 10	Month 11	Month 12
Process 5: Survey Feedback on team effectiveness		Process 4: Operational Review

7

MEASURING PERFORMANCE

While traditional leaders and their departments have historically been evaluated solely on the extent to which they achieve results, the effectiveness of the facilitative organization is more properly assessed in terms of two separate but interconnected dimensions.

Performance Dimensions of the Facilitative Organization

When an organization operates in the facilitative mode, it aims to be effective in two interconnected dimensions. The first dimension continues to be the extent to which expected outcomes are achieved. The important new element is the extent to which effective processes were applied. It thus recognizes the vital role of process to the overall success of any endeavor and ultimately to the health of the entire organization.

Dimensions for Assessing Effectiveness in the Facilitative Organization

Dimension 1: The extent to which expected outcomes are achieved

Dimension 2: The extent to which effective processes are applied

---

When both the results and the process elements are used to guide evaluations, a more balanced picture of performance emerges:

Performance Categories for the Results Dimension

- The extent to which outcomes match expectations
- The rate of return on investment
- Whether results were a breakthrough
- Timeliness of delivery
- Budget management
- Whether the customer's needs were met
- Impact on the operation
- Overall impact on the organization

Performance Categories for the Process Dimension

- Clarity of parameters
- Presence of clear and logical steps
- Effectiveness of the team
- Quality of communications
- Effectiveness of meetings
- Stakeholder involvement
- Levels of collaboration
- Effectiveness of the leader

Assessing the Dimensions

The instruments that follow feature questions useful to assess each of these dimensions. It is suggested that both elements be given equal weight based on the cause and effect premise that these dimensions are intimately linked and that superior results can be achieved only when both dimensions drive performance.

Performance Measures for the Results Dimension

1. To what extent did the outcomes match expectations?   _____

    1 = They did not match expectations at all.

    2 = Expectations were somewhat met.

    3 = Expectations were mostly met.

    4 = Expectations were totally met.

    5 = Expectations were exceeded.

2. Rate the return on investment.   _____

    1 = The initial investment was lost.

    2 = The return on investment was low.

    3 = The return on investment was moderate.

    4 = The return on investment was high.

    5 = The return on investment was outstanding.

3. To what extent were the outcomes a breakthrough?   _____

    1 = The outcomes were conventional.

    2 = The outcomes were somewhat innovative.

    3 = The outcomes were quite innovative.

    4 = The outcomes were very innovative.

    5 = The outcomes were a major creative breakthrough.

4. To what extent were results delivered on time?   _____

    1 = They were delivered very late.

    2 = They were delivered slightly late.

    3 = They were delivered on time.

    4 = They were delivered slightly ahead of time.

    5 = They were delivered extremely rapidly.

(Continued)

5. How well was the budget managed?   _____

    1 = The initiative came in seriously over budget.

    2 = The initiative came in slightly over budget.

    3 = The initiative came in on budget.

    4 = The initiative came in slightly under budget.

    5 = The initiative came in well under budget.

6. To what extent were the customer's requirements met?   _____

    1 = Customer expectations were not met at all.

    2 = Customer expectations were somewhat met.

    3 = Customer expectations were mostly met.

    4 = Customer expectations were totally met.

    5 = Customer expectations were exceeded.

7. To what extent did the initiative improve the operation? _____

    1 = The operation was made worse.

    2 = The operation was made slightly worse.

    3 = The operation is unchanged.

    4 = The operation has been slightly improved.

    5 = The operation has been greatly improved.

8. To what extent did the outcomes improve the overall   _____
organization?

    1 = It made us worse.

    2 = It has had no impact.

    3 = It has made us slightly better.

    4 = It has made us much better.

    5 = It has sparked a major and positive transformation.

Total score in the results dimension (maximum = 40)   _____

Performance Measures for the Process Dimension

1. To what extent did the initiative operate with clear   ____
   parameters?

   > 1 = The parameters were never clear.
   >
   > 2 = The parameters were fairly clear.
   >
   > 3 = The parameters were mostly clear.
   >
   > 4 = The parameters were always clear.
   >
   > 5 = The parameters were regularly reviewed and updated.

2. To what extent did the initiative operate with clear   ____
   and logical processes?

   > 1 = Things seemed to operate largely ad hoc.
   >
   > 2 = There were some processes in place for specific tasks.
   >
   > 3 = There were processes in place for most tasks.
   >
   > 4 = There were clear and logical processes in place for all
   >   tasks.
   >
   > 5 = There were clear and logical processes in place, and
   >   these were reviewed from time to time to ensure their
   >   effectiveness.

3. To what extent was a cohesive and collaborative   ____
   team created?

   > 1 = The project team was totally dysfunctional.
   >
   > 2 = Members periodically acted like a team.
   >
   > 3 = Members acted like a team most of the time.
   >
   > 4 = Members became a fairly effective team.
   >
   > 5 = Members became a high-performance team.

(Continued)

4. To what extent were communications effective?   _____

   1 = No one ever seemed to know what was going on.

   2 = Some people had information on some matters.

   3 = Communications seemed adequate most of the time.

   4 = Communications were good.

   5 = Communications were excellent and worked in multiple directions.

5. How efficient and effective were the meetings?   _____

   1 = Meeting were totally unstructured and a waste of time.

   2 = Some meetings seemed to work.

   3 = Most meetings were well organized and effective.

   4 = All meetings were well planned and productive.

   5 = Staff meetings were well planned and productive, and they provided a forum for creative dialogue.

6. To what extent were important stakeholders involved?   _____

   1 = What stakeholders?

   2 = Stakeholders were rarely consulted and involved.

   3 = A few stakeholders were consulted and involved.

   4 = Most stakeholders were consulted and involved.

   5 = Stakeholders were consulted and made a part of the process at every step that involved them.

7. To what extent are the results indicative of true collaboration?   _____

   1 = A few people dominated, while other voices were not heard.

   2 = There were attempts at collaboration.

   3 = There was collaboration on some matters.

   4 = There was a lot of collaboration.

   5 = The results truly reflect an outcome that we all contributed to and can live with.

8. How effectively did the leader perform?   _____

   1 = The leader was totally ineffective and lost the confidence of all of the team members.

   2 = The leader was largely ineffective and lost the confidence of some of the team members.

   3 = The leader had some strengths and performed some functions well.

   4 = The team leader had many strengths and consistently performed well.

   5 = The team leader was extremely skilled and inspired members to achieve outstanding results.

Total score in the process dimension (maximum = 40)   _____

Interpreting the Results

Post tabulated results on the Performance Measure Graph to iden-tify the quadrant that describes overall performance:

PERFORMANCE MEASURE GRAPH

Quadrant 1: Low results and low process. Organizations and initiatives that score in this quadrant have failed to achieve their expected results. They also operated in an unstructured manner and with low levels of both collaboration and trust.

Quadrant 2: Low results but high process. Organizations and initiatives that score in this quadrant have failed to achieve their expected results. They did, however, operate with effective processes and created a collaborative and trusting environment.

Quadrant 3: High results but low process. Organizations and initiatives that score in this quadrant have achieved their expected results. They did this despite the fact that they operated without effective processes and failed to create a collaborative and trusting environment.

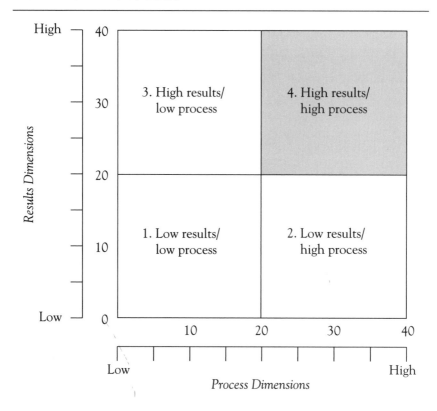

Quadrant 4: High results and high process. Organizations and initiatives that score in this quadrant have achieved their expected results. They operated with effective processes and created a collaborative and trusting environment.

When a team or initiative receives performance scores that place it in quadrant 1, this is indicative of total failure in both the results and process dimensions, an unacceptable performance.

Scores that place a team or initiative in quadrant 2 are also unacceptable, since no one, not even a relationship-oriented leader, seeks to create a happy team that can't get anything done.

Receiving scores in quadrant 3 may have been acceptable in another era, but today no one should be rewarded for achieving results attained through unstructured chaos and fractured teams.

Scoring in quadrant 4 is the optimal outcome since it indicates that the team was effective in both dimensions. First and foremost, above-average results were achieved. Second, processes and relationships were effective.

Teams and initiatives that score in quadrant 4 have created a culture of collaboration that exerts a positive influence on the rest of their organization. Achieving scores in this quadrant also indicates that team members have gained leadership skills that they can deploy in other areas.

> It's essential to measure both results and processes.

When teams pay attention to both the task and process elements of their work, they are far more likely to succeed, and a more accurate picture of their true effectiveness emerges.

Measuring Individual Performance

Facilitative organizations need to implement new ways of measuring individual performance. While traditional organizations conduct mostly top-down performance appraisals, facilitative organizations need to use performance review activities in which feedback flows both upward and across.

Two separate but compatible personal performance evaluation instruments are provided here. The first describes the observable behaviors of the facilitative leader. The second focuses on the behaviors of team members. Since these two roles are synergistically linked and completely interdependent, it would be a mistake to conduct only one of these assessments.

While traditional organizations keep performance appraisal results confidential, facilitative organizations use this information to start open conversations aimed at furthering learning and development.

Facilitative Leader Index

Effective facilitative leaders consistently display the behaviors described below. Reflect on your leader, and provide a rating for each item on a 1–5 scale:

1 = never does this (0–20 percent of the time)

2 = very rarely does this (20–40 percent of the time)

3 = sometimes does this (40–60 percent of the time)

4 = often does this (60–80 percent of the time)

5 = almost always does this (80–100 percent of the time)

1. Empowering others: The extent to which the leader:

   _____ Systematically distributes decision-making authority to encourage people to take charge and assume responsibility for outcomes.

   _____ Involves team members in decision making on issues that affect them and their work.

   _____ Encourages team members to be self-managing.

   _____ Respects the knowledge and expertise of members and supports their decisions.

2. Creating a collaborative environment: The extent to which the leader:

   _____ Builds alignment by enrolling everyone in building a shared vision of the future.

   _____ Facilitates the development of norms that help create a collaborative and supportive culture.

   _____ Ensures that everyone's input is heard and valued.

   _____ Builds consensus whenever substantive decisions need to be made.

3. Fostering creativity: the extent to which the leader:

_____ Encourages innovation by creating an atmosphere where new ideas are welcomed and valued.

_____ Encourages team members to form networks and explore new synergies.

_____ Is willing to take risks and try new ideas.

_____ Doesn't hesitate to champion new ideas with upper management.

4. Operating with transparency: The extent to which the leader:

_____ Spends time and energy creating an atmosphere of openness and trust.

_____ Works hard to ensure that the team has the information it needs about the organization, its policies, and its plans.

_____ Takes time with each team member to understand his or her specific information needs and establish effective lines of communication.

_____ Structures all interactions to encourage multidirectional information flow.

5. Taking a systems approach: The extent to which the leader:

_____ Ensures that the objectives of the team are relevant to and connected with the strategic goals of the organization and other key stakeholders.

_____ Ensures that the roles and responsibilities of each team member are defined.

_____ Helps people see the connection between their work and broader impacts.

_____ Helps the team members identify strategic alliances and other important linkages.

(Continued)

6. Harnessing feedback: The extent to which the leader:

____ Puts mechanisms in place so that people can safely give feedback about both the effectiveness of relationships and the overall operation.

____ Creates mechanisms so that all team members (including the leader) receive periodic feedback concerning their performance.

____ Makes sure that initiatives are debriefed and become opportunities for learning.

____ Monitors team performance and takes steps to continuously improve group effectiveness.

7. Developing personal capacity: The extent to which the leader:

____ Encourages team members to identify their special talents and create a personal development plan.

____ Knows the special skills and talents of each team member and consistently taps into that knowledge base.

____ Works to provide team members with the training and work experiences they need in order to achieve their development goals.

____ Coaches members who need to overcome personal performance issues.

8. Acting as a model: The extent to which the leader:

____ Uses language and behaviors consistent with being in a facilitative mode.

____ Manages the team's work in a structured and organized manner.

____ Downplays status and treats everyone on the team like a colleague and valued partner.

____ Acts on feedback in order to develop himself or herself personally and professionally.

____ Total score (maximum possible score = 160)

Index Scorecard

Optimal	120–160
Effective	80–119
Satisfactory	40–79
Ineffective	0–39

Category Scores

Empowering others	____
Creating a collaborative environment	____
Fostering creativity	____
Operating with transparency	____
Taking a systems approach	____
Harnessing feedback	____
Developing personal capacity	____
Acting as a model	____

The maximum score for each category is 20.

Empowered Partner Index

Facilitative leaders can succeed only if all team members see themselves as full and equal partners in the enterprise. Team members are most effective when they exhibit the behaviors described in this instrument. Reflect on a specific team member, and provide him or her with specific feedback using this rating chart:

1 = never does this (0–20 percent of the time)
2 = very rarely does this (20–40 percent of the time)
3 = sometimes does this (40–60 percent of the time)
4 = often does this (60–80 percent of the time)
5 = almost always does this (80–100 percent of the time)

1. Taking responsibility: The extent to which the member:

_____ Contributes to the development of the vision and goals that guide the team.

_____ Accepts increased levels of empowerment and willingly takes on expanded responsibilities.

_____ Accepts the consequences associated with achieving specific outcomes.

_____ Tries to solve problems before bringing them to anyone else.

_____ Shares ideas in meetings and supports team decisions.

_____ Manages work in accordance with the highest standards of the profession.

2. Working with discipline: The extent to which the member:

_____ Maintains a detailed set of work objectives that mesh with the vision, goals, and objectives of the team.

_____ Works independently to self-manage daily activities.

_____ Monitors and reports on personal progress in a clear and timely manner.

_____ Willingly takes initiative and makes decisions without waiting for direction.

_____ Demonstrates competence and commitment in doing his or her work.

_____ Communicates continuously with the leader, teammates, and other stakeholders to keep everyone informed.

3. Supporting others: The extent to which the member:

_____ Acts like a team player, always putting *we* before *I*.

_____ Keeps commitments to avoid letting down other members of the team.

_____ Refrains from spreading gossip about teammates or sharing team confidences with people outside the team.

_____ Refrains from engaging in interpersonal conflict and seeks to solve differences through dialogue instead.

_____ Readily takes on a fair share of the work that needs to be done.

_____ Is always willing to lend a hand to teammates who need help.

4. Pursuing personal development: The extent to which the member:

_____ Is active in acquiring the skills needed to achieve superior results.

_____ Gladly takes on challenging, new assignments that let him or her gain new skills.

_____ Willingly shares his or her knowledge and coaches teammates.

_____ Seeks knowledge of and exposure to other functions and teams.

_____ Objectively assesses his or her work to look for lessons and improvement ideas.

_____ Is open to feedback and makes adjustments to behavior.

(Continued)

5. Managing personal conduct: The extent to which the member:

_____ Is optimistic and takes a can-do approach to challenges.

_____ Extends a trusting and positive attitude toward colleagues, leaders, and the organization.

_____ Respects and adheres to the rules set by the team.

_____ Listens carefully and tries to understand the views of others, especially when they don't agree with him or her.

_____ Respects differences in the backgrounds and personalities of individuals on the team.

_____ Is willing to step into the leadership role whenever the need arises.

_____ Total score (maximum possible score = 150)

Index Scorecard

Optimal	114–150
Effective	76–113
Satisfactory	38–75
Ineffective	0–37

Category Scores

Taking responsibility	_____
Working with discipline	_____
Supporting others	_____
Pursuing personal development	_____
Personal conduct	_____

The maximum score in each category is 30.

Epilogue:
Life in a Facilitative Organization

When organizations create the right supporting conditions and when masterful facilitative leaders are deployed in the right settings, members will experience a workplace that is organized, efficient, responsive, cooperative, and creative.

Team members will also notice these defining features:

• There is much more structure than in the traditional workplace. Not only are all of the operational elements planned out as they would be in any other well-run project, but the process and relationship elements are also systematically managed. There is a schedule whereby both task and relationship elements are routinely reviewed and improved.

• Meetings are highly efficient. There are no more free-wheeling, unplanned discussions where decisions are made by those who have rank or whoever talks the most. Meetings are timed and actively facilitated. The meeting format used matches the communication needs of the group.

• Relationships are cultivated. Members regularly engage in structured conversations to build and maintain effective working relationships. Rifts, power struggles, cliques, and infighting are never ignored. Interventions and mediations are used at the first signs of strife to restore cooperation.

• Learning is important. There are continuous feedback loops to review past activities to glean lessons learned and spark greater creativity. Other organizations are studied and benchmarked against. Team members take turns teaching so that knowledge is shared.

• Everyone leads. The combination of skilled workers and elevated levels of empowerment creates a situation where members take the lead. This sense of being in charge energizes staff and feeds the cycle of success.

Given the continuing proliferation of network teams, there is every reason to be optimistic that all successful organizations will soon describe themselves as being facilitative. When this happens, facilitative leaders will be so common that when the average person is asked to describe what a leader is, they will say, "Someone who creates the conditions in which people can be great."

Appendix A: Organizational Readiness Assessment

In order for facilitative leadership to be successful, specific support mechanisms must be in place. This assessment can be used to raise awareness of gaps and can serve as a starting point for planning discussions aimed at creating the needed support mechanisms.

Provide a rating for each item using the following scale:

1 = totally   2 = disagree   3 = not sure   4 = agree   5 = totally
   disagree   agree

1. We have a clear understanding of the nature of facilitative leadership and firmly believe that this role is critically important to the long-term success of the organization. _____

2. We can identify situations where facilitative leadership is a good fit. _____

3. We accept that participative management may be a significant cultural change that will require some adjustment and investment. _____

4. Individual upper managers are willing to shift their personal style to one that is more collaborative and inclusive to send a congruent cultural message. _____

5. We are prepared to increase the empowerment of teams that demonstrate their readiness for increased accountability. _____

6. Upper managers accept that effective collaboration requires that they be open to periodically receiving feedback from other parts of the organization. _____

7. We are prepared to simplify procedures and remove blocks that might slow progress or stifle creativity. _____

8. Upper managers are ready to act as champions to leaders when they need help getting things done. _____

9. We have put in place adequate funds to provide the training and development that facilitative leaders require. _____

10. We have adjusted our leadership position descriptions to include the competencies of the facilitative leader to ensure that qualified people are hired for these positions. _____

11. We have altered our criteria for evaluating leaders to reflect the competencies of the facilitative leader. _____

12. We have adjusted our criteria for rewarding and promoting leaders to ensure that facilitative leaders are encouraged and respected. _____

Our Organizational Readiness Scorecard (maximum = 60)   _____

Scorecard

Optimal readiness	45–60
Somewhat ready	30–44
Largely unready	15–29
Totally unready	0–14

Interpreting the Results

Optimal readiness: Organizations scoring in this range fully understand the concept of facilitative leadership and are aware of the cultural implications. The critical support elements such as upper management support, targeted training programs, and willingness to empower, receive feedback, and use appropriate appraisal and pay mechanisms have been put in place. The conditions are advantageous for the deployment of facilitative leaders.

Somewhat ready: Organizations in this range have many of the key support mechanisms in place; however, some elements have not received the attention they need, and more planning is needed.

Largely unready: Organizations in this range are not ready to support facilitative leadership but can create the right conditions if they address the items that received low ratings.

Totally unready: Organizations in this range should not implement this approach to leadership without investing time and energy to create the requisite conditions.

Elements that received high scores:

Elements that scored low and need to be addressed:

Appendix B:
Facilitation Skills Self-Assessment

Identify your current level of facilitation mastery by reviewing the descriptions and competencies that follow. The descriptions and competencies are arranged in three levels:

Level I—consists of the core skills required to lead routine discussions and manage meetings effectively

Level II—consists of the ability to design complex decision processes and manage difficult situations

Level III—involves designing and leading interventions

Provide a rating for each item using the following scale:

1 = totally   2 = disagree   3 = not sure   4 = agree   5 = totally
   disagree   agree

Level I: Basic Competencies

1. I understand the concepts, values, and beliefs underpinning facilitation. ____

2. I'm aware of what to do at the start, middle, and end of a facilitation. ____

From Bens, I. *Advanced Facilitation Strategies*. San Francisco: Jossey-Bass, 2005.

3. I'm skilled at active listening, paraphrasing, questioning, and summarizing key points. _____

4. I'm able to manage time and maintain a good pace. _____

5. I know techniques for encouraging active participation and generating ideas. _____

6. I know how to create and then use group norms to encourage effective behaviors. _____

7. I can make clear notes that accurately reflect what members have said. _____

8. I'm familiar with the core process tools used to structure participative group discussions. _____

9. I understand the differences among various decision-making tools and know when to use each one. _____

10. I understand how to help a group achieve consensus and gain closure. _____

11. I'm skilled at offering constructive feedback to groups and am comfortable accepting personal feedback. _____

12. I know the key components of an effective meeting design and can create a detailed agenda. _____

13. I know how to ask good probing questions that challenge assumptions in a nonthreatening way. _____

14. I know when and how to conduct periodic process checks. _____

15. I know how to use a variety of exit surveys to improve meeting effectiveness. _____

Level II: Intermediate Competencies

16. I know how to use surveys and conduct interviews to assess group needs and interests. _____

17. I can design meetings for a variety of purposes and can adjust my designs in midstream if necessary. _____

18. I know strategies to create a safe environment and gain buy-in from reluctant participants. _____

19. I can deal with resistance nondefensively, even when it's aimed at me personally. _____

20. I know the signs of groupthink and can structure discussions to overcome it. _____

21. I'm skilled at asking complex probing questions that help members uncover underlying issues and information. _____

22. I can recognize the signs of group tension or conflict and do not hesitate to offer that insight to groups. _____

23. I'm able to appropriately and assertively intervene in order to redirect ineffective behavior. _____

24. I'm able to articulate both sides of an issue, then offer a process to reframe the conversation. _____

25. I'm able to hear and then consolidate ideas from a mass of information and create coherent summaries. _____

26. I can recognize when decision processes are polarized and know how to restructure them so they're collaborative. _____

27. I possess tools to help groups out of decision deadlocks. _____

28. I understand the team development process and know how to implement a variety of team-building activities. _____

29. I'm sensitive to the interests, needs, and concerns of individuals from different cultural backgrounds and from various levels and functions in the organization. _____

30. I'm sufficiently versed in process responses that I never lose my neutrality even during difficult conversations. _____

Level III: Advanced Competencies

31. I have a personal philosophy of facilitation that guides my work. _____

32. I'm aware of strategies for negotiating the power I need in order to be effective in any situation. _____

33. I understand the theories and primary methodologies of organization development. _____

34. I'm aware of the steps that make up the core processes that facilitators are asked to apply. _____

35. I'm aware of change management models and can use them to design and implement complex change activities. _____

36. I know how to design and facilitate various strategic and business planning discussions. _____

37. I know the steps in the main process tools that are part of process improvement efforts, such as process mapping. _____

38. I'm skilled at designing and implementing surveys. _____

39. I'm skilled at using survey feedback to involve teammates to interpret their own data and identify actions. _____

40. I'm able to design and implement interpersonal and intergroup conflict interventions to settle contentious issues. _____

41. I'm aware of the steps in the coaching process and know how to use coaching to help individuals and teams. _____

42. I'm able to deal comfortably with upper management both individually and in group settings. _____

43. I know how to negotiate the power and authority levels I need in order to be effective. _____

44. I'm able to design complex one- and two-day
   meetings and retreats to achieve specific outcomes.   _____

Skills and competencies that I currently possess:

Skills and competencies that I would like to develop further:

Further Reading

Anderson, T. D. *Transforming Leadership*. Amherst, Mass.: HRD Press, 1992.

Argyris, C. *Intervention Theory and Method*. Reading, Mass.: Addison-Wesley, 1970.

Argyris, C., Putnam, R., and Smith, D. M. *Action Science*. San Francisco: Jossey-Bass, 1985.

Autry, J. A. *The Servant Leader*. Roseville, Calif.: Prima Publishing, 2001.

Axelrod, R. *The Evolution of Cooperation*. New York: Basic Books, 1984.

Beckhard, R. "The Confrontation Meeting." *Harvard Business Review*, 1967, 4, 149–155.

Beckhard, R. *Organization Development: Strategies and Models*. Reading, Mass.: Addison-Wesley, 1969.

Beckhard, R., and Harris, R. *Organizational Transitions: Managing Complex Change*. (2nd ed.) Reading, Mass.: Addison-Wesley, 1987.

Belasco, J., and Stayer, R. *Flight of the Buffalo*. New York: Warner, 1993.

Bennis, W. *Why Leaders Can't Lead*. San Francisco: Jossey-Bass, 1989.

Bennis, W., and Goldsmith, J. *Learning to Lead*. New York: Perseus Books, 2003.

Bennis, W., and Nanus, B. *Leaders: The Strategies for Taking Charge*. New York: HarperCollins, 1985.

Bennis, W., Spreitzer, G. M., and Cummings, T. G. *The Future of Leadership*. San Francisco: Jossey-Bass, 2001.

Bens, I. *Advanced Facilitation Strategies*. San Francisco: Jossey-Bass, 2005.

Bens, I. *Facilitating with Ease!* (2nd ed.) San Francisco: Jossey-Bass, 2005.

Blake, R. R., Shepared, H., and Mouton, J. S. *Managing Intergroup Conflict in Industry*. Houston: Gulf Publishing, 1965.

Block, P. *The Empowered Manager*. San Francisco: Jossey-Bass, 1990.

Block, P. *Stewardship*. San Francisco: Berrett-Koehler, 1993.

Bracken, D. W., Timmreck, C. W., and Church, A. H. (eds.). *The Handbook of Multi-Source Feedback*. San Francisco: Jossey-Bass, 2001.

Bradford, L. P. (ed.). *Group Development*. San Diego, Calif.: University Associates, 1978.

Brown, S., and Fisher, R. *Getting Together*. New York: Penguin, 1992.

Burns, J. M. *Leadership*. New York: HarperCollins, 1978.

Byham, W. C., and Cox, J. *Zapp! The Lightning of Empowerment.* New York: Ballantine Books, 1988.

Carr, C., *Team Leader's Problem Solver.* Upper Saddle River, N.J.: Prentice Hall, 1996.

Dalkey, N. *The Delphi Method: An Experimental Study of Group Opinion.* Santa Monica, Calif.: Rand, 1969.

De Pree, M. *Leadership Is an Art.* New York: Doubleday, 1989.

Dimock, H. G. *Leadership and Group Development.* San Diego, Calif.: University Associates, 1984.

Dotlich, D., and Cairo, P. *Action Coaching.* San Francisco: Jossey-Bass, 1999.

Duarte, D. L., and Snyder, N. T. *Mastering Virtual Teams.* (2nd ed.) San Francisco: Jossey-Bass, 2001.

Dyer, W. G. *Team Building: Issues and Alternatives.* Reading, Mass.: Addison-Wesley, 1977.

Dyer, W. G. *Team Building.* (2nd ed.) Reading, Mass.: Addison-Wesley, 1987.

Eggleton, H. C., and Rice, J. C. *The Fieldbook of Team Interventions.* Amherst, Mass.: HRD Press, 1996.

Fairhurst, G., and Sarr, R. *The Art of Framing.* San Francisco: Jossey-Bass, 1996.

Fink, A. *The Survey Handbook.* Thousand Oaks, Calif.: Sage, 1995.

Finzel, H. *The Top Ten Mistakes Leaders Make.* Colorado Springs: Cook Communications, 2000.

Fisher, A. B. *Small Group Decision Making: Communication and Group Process.* New York: McGraw-Hill, 1974.

Forsyth, D. R. *Group Dynamics.* Pacific Grove, Calif.: Brooks/Cole, 1990.

Fox, J. J. *How to Become a Great Boss.* New York: Hyperion Publishing, 2002.

Francis, D., and Woodcock, M. *Unblocking Organizational Values.* San Diego, Calif.: University Associates, 1990.

Francis, D., and Young, D. *Improving Work Groups: A Practical Manual for Team Building.* San Francisco: Jossey-Bass/Pfeiffer, 1992.

French, W., and Bell, C., Jr. *Organization Development: Behavioral Science Interventions for Organization Improvement.* (3rd ed.) Upper Saddle River, N.J.: Prentice Hall, 1990.

Hargrove, R. *Masterful Coaching.* San Francisco: Jossey-Bass/Pfeiffer, 1995.

Harrison, R. "Choosing the Depth of Organizational Intervention." *Journal of Applied Behavioral Science,* 1970, 6, 182–202.

Hart, L. B. *Faultless Facilitation.* Amherst, Mass.: HRD Press, 1992.

Heron, J. *Group Facilitation: Theories and Models for Practice.* London: Kogan Page, 1993.

Hersey, P., and Blanchard, K. *The Situational Leadership Model.* San Francisco: Jossey-Bass/Pfeiffer, 1968.

Hersey, P., and Blanchard, K. *Management of Organizational Behavior: Utilizing Human Resources.* (4th ed.) Upper Saddle River, N.J.: Prentice Hall, 1982.

Hesselbein, F., Goldsmith, M., and Beckhard, R. (eds.). *The Organization of the Future*. San Francisco: Jossey-Bass, 1997.

Higgs, A. C., and Ashworth, S. D. *Organizational Surveys: Tools for Assessment and Change*. San Francisco: Jossey-Bass, 1996.

Howell, J. L. *Tools for Facilitating Team Meetings*. Seattle: Integrity Publishing, 1995.

Hunsaker, P., and Alessandra, A. *The Art of Managing People*. Upper Saddle River, N.J.: Prentice Hall, 1980.

Johnson, S. *Who Moved My Cheese?* New York: Penguin Putnam, 1998.

Jones, J. E., and Bearley, W. K. *Surveying Employees: A Practical Guidebook*. Amherst, Mass.: HRD Press, 1995.

Kaner, S. *Facilitator's Guide to Participatory Decision-Making*. Philadelphia: New Society Publishers, 1996.

Katzenbach, J., and Smith, D. *The Wisdom of Teams*. New York: HarperCollins, 1993.

Kaufman, R. *Identifying and Solving Problems*. San Diego, Calif.: University Associates, 1976.

Kayser, T. A. *Mining Group Gold*. Sequido, Calif.: Serif Publishing, 1990.

Keating, C. J. *Dealing with Difficult People*. New York: Paulist Press, 1984.

Kindler, H. S. *Managing Disagreement Constructively*. Los Altos, Calif.: Crisp Publications, 1988.

Kinlaw, D. C. *Team-Managed Facilitation*. San Francisco: Jossey-Bass/Pfeiffer, 1993.

Kouzes, J., and Posner, B. *The Leadership Challenge*. San Francisco: Jossey-Bass, 1987.

Laborde, G. *Influencing with Integrity*. Palo Alto, Calif.: Syntony Publishing, 1984.

Lawler, E. E. *High Involvement Management*. San Francisco: Jossey-Bass, 1986.

Leigh, A., and Maynard, M. *Leading Your Team*. London: Nicholas Brealey, 1995.

Levine, S. *Getting Resolution: Turning Conflict into Collaboration*. San Francisco: Berrett-Koehler, 1999.

Likert, R. *New Patterns of Management*. New York: McGraw-Hill, 1967.

Likert, R., and Likert, J. G. *New Ways of Managing Conflict*. New York: McGraw-Hill, 1976.

Lippitt, G., and Lippitt, R. *The Consulting Process in Action*. (2nd ed.) San Francisco: Jossey-Bass, 1986.

Locke, E., and Latham, G. *Goal Setting*. Upper Saddle River, N.J.: Prentice Hall, 1984.

McGregor, D. *The Human Side of Enterprise*. New York: McGraw-Hill, 1960.

McPherson, J. H. *The People, the Problems and the Problem-Solving Methods*. Midland, Mich.: Pendell Company, 1967.

Means, J., and Adams, T. *Facilitating the Project Lifecycle*. San Francisco: Jossey-Bass, 2005.

Mindell, P. *How to Say IT for Executives*. New York: Prentice Hall Press, 2005.

Mosvick, R., and Nelson, R. *We've Got to Start Meeting Like This!* Upper Saddle River, N.J.: Scott, Foresman, 1987.

Nadler, D. A. *Feedback and Organization Development: Using Data-Based Methods.* Reading, Mass.: Addison-Wesley, 1977.

Nelson, B. *1001 Ways to Energize Employees.* New York: Workman Publishing, 1997.

Nelson, B., and Spitzer, D. *The 1001 Rewards and Recognition Fieldbook.* New York: Workman Publishing, 2003.

Owen, H. *Open Space Technology: A User's Guide.* Potomac, Md.: Abbott Press, 1992.

Peters, T. J., and Waterman, R. H. *In Search of Excellence: Lessons from America's Best Run Companies.* New York: Warner, 1984.

Pfeiffer, J. W., and Jones, J. E. *A Handbook of Structured Experiences for Human Relations Training.* San Francisco: Jossey-Bass/Pfeiffer, 1972.

Ray, G. R. *The Facilitative Leader.* Upper Saddle River, N.J.: Prentice Hall, 1999.

Reddy, B. *Intervention Skills: Process Consultation for Small Groups and Teams.* San Francisco: Jossey-Bass/Pfeiffer, 1994.

Rees, F. *How to Lead Work Teams.* San Francisco: Jossey-Bass/Pfeiffer, 1991.

Rees, F. *The Facilitator Excellence Handbook.* San Francisco: Jossey-Bass/Pfeiffer, 1998.

Saint, S., and Lawson, J. R. *Rules for Reaching Consensus.* San Francisco: Jossey-Bass/Pfeiffer, 1994.

Sashkin, M., and Kiser, K. J. *Putting Total Quality to Work.* San Francisco: Berrett-Koehler, 1993.

Sashkin, M., and Sashkin, M. *Leadership That Matters.* San Francisco: Berrett-Koehler, 2002.

Schein, E. H. *Process Consultation: Its Role in Organization Development.* Reading, Mass.: Addison-Wesley, 1969.

Schein, E. H. *Organizational Culture and Leadership.* (2nd ed.) San Francisco: Jossey-Bass, 1992.

Scholtes, P. R. *The Leader's Handbook.* New York: McGraw-Hill, 1998.

Schutz, W. C. *The Interpersonal Underworld.* Palo Alto, Calif.: Science and Behavior Books, 1996.

Senge, P. M. *The Fifth Discipline.* New York: Doubleday, 1990.

Shonk, J. H. *Team Based Organizations.* New York: Irwin, 1992.

Stanfield, R. B. (ed.). *The Art of Focused Conversation.* Toronto, Canada: ICA Canada, 2000.

Staub, R. E. II. *The Heart of Leadership.* Greensboro, N.C.: Staub Leadership Publishing, 2002.

Strachen, D. *Questions That Work.* Ottawa, Canada: ST Press, 2001.

Tagliere, D. A. *How to Meet, Think and Work to Consensus.* San Francisco: Jossey-Bass/Pfeiffer, 1992.

Tichy, N. M. *The Leadership Engine.* New York: HarperCollins, 2002.

Tuckman, B. W. "Developmental Sequence in Small Groups." *Psychological Bulletin*, 1965, *63*, 384–399.

Van Gundy, A. B. *Techniques of Structured Problem Solving.* New York: Van Nostrand Reinhold, 1981.

Vengel, A. *The Influence Edge: How to Persuade Others to Help You Achieve Your Goals.* San Francisco: Berrett-Koehler, 1998.

Vroom, V. H., and Yetton, P. W. *Leadership and Decision Making.* Pittsburgh, Pa.: University of Pittsburgh Press, 1973.

Weaver, R. G., and Farrell, J. D. *Managers as Facilitators.* San Francisco: Berrett-Koehler, 1997.

Weisbord, M. M. *Productive Workplaces.* San Francisco: Jossey-Bass, 1991.

Weisbord, M. R. *Organizational Diagnosis: A Workbook of Theory and Practice.* Reading, Mass.: Addison-Wesley, 1995.

Wellins, R. S., Byham, W. C., and Wilson, J. M. *Empowered Teams.* San Francisco: Jossey-Bass, 1991.

Wellins, R. S., Schaff, D., and Shomo, K. H. *Succeeding with Teams.* Minneapolis, Minn.: Lakewood Books, 1994.

Wheatley, M. J. *Leadership and the New Science: Learning About Organizations from an Orderly Universe.* San Francisco: Berrett-Koehler, 1992.

Whitmore, J. *Coaching for Performance.* San Francisco: Jossey-Bass/Pfeiffer, 1992.

Wilson, J. M., George, J., and Wellins, S. *Leadership Trapeze: Strategies for Leadership in Team-Based Organizations.* San Francisco: Jossey-Bass, 1994.

Wilson, P. H. *The Facilitative Way.* Shawnee Mission, Kans.: TeamTech Press, 2003.

Wood, J. T., Phillips, G. M., and Pederson, D. J. *Group Discussion: A Practical Guide to Participation and Leadership.* (2nd ed.) New York: HarperCollins, 1986.

Zander, A. *Making Groups Effective.* San Francisco: Jossey-Bass, 1983.

Index